Puffin Books
Editor: Kaye Webb

ALL ABOUT THE BULLERBY CHILDREN

The Bullerby children were the six children who lived in three farms which stood side by side in a tiny hamlet in Sweden called Bullerby. Lisa, who tells these stories, lived in the middle house with her two big brothers Lars and Pip. Olaf lived on one side, and Britta and Anna on the other.

Some of the stories Lisa tells are about things that only happen in Sweden: like the way the whole family wake up a birthday child with a tray with a birthday cake, flowers and a cup of hot chocolate on it; or their special Christmas customs; but most of the other adventures could have happened almost anywhere. For instance, there was the time the teacher told poor Olaf to pull out his wobbly tooth, the time the girls tried sleeping out in the barn, Aunt Jenny's Christmas party when *fourteen* children all slept the night on the floor in a row, and the fun the girls had when they looked after Olaf's naughty baby sister for the day.

All these friendly, funny, down-to-earth stories are beautifully told by the well-known Swedish writer, Astrid Lindgren. Two more of her books, *The Mischievous Martens* and *Lotta Leaves Home*, are also published in a Young Puffin under the title *Lotta.*

For readers of six to eight.

ASTRID LINDGREN

ALL ABOUT THE BULLERBY CHILDREN

ILLUSTRATED BY
ILON WIKLAND

Puffin Books

Puffin Books: A Division of
Penguin Books Ltd, Harmondsworth,
Middlesex, England
Penguin Books Australia Ltd, Ringwood,
Victoria, Australia
Penguin Books (N.Z.) Ltd,
182–190 Wairau Road, Auckland 10, New Zealand

The stories in this volume were first published in
Sweden in *Alla Vi Barn i Bullerbyn* and *Bullerby Boken*
First published in Great Britain 1963, 1964, 1965

Stories nos. 1–10 are from *The Six Bullerby Children*
Translated by Evelyn Ramsden

Stories nos. 16–21, 26, 28, 29 are from *Cherry Time at Bullerby*
Stories nos. 11–15, 22–25, 27 are from *Happy Days at Bullerby*
Both translated by Florence Lamborn

This collection first published by Methuen 1970
Published in Puffin Books 1974

Made and printed in Great Britain by
Richard Clay (The Chaucer Press) Ltd
Bungay, Suffolk
Set in Monotype Bembo

Contents

1. The three farms

My name is Lisa, and I'm a girl – but of course you can tell that from my name. I'm seven years old, rising eight.

Sometimes Mother says: 'You're getting such a big girl now that you can help me with the washing-up.' But then Lars and Pip say: 'We don't want any babies playing Indians with us. You're much too small.'

And so I begin to wonder whether I am big or small, because some people say I am a big girl and some that I am a small girl. Perhaps I am just right!

Lars and Pip are my brothers. Lars is nine years old and Pip is eight. Lars is very strong and can run much faster than I can, but I can run as fast as Pip. Sometimes, when the boys don't want me to go with them, Lars holds me while Pip runs away so that he can get ahead. And then Lars lets go of me and runs off with Pip, leaving me behind, which he does very easily. I haven't got a sister, which is a pity. Boys are so noisy.

We live on a farm called the Middle Farm, because it lies exactly midway between two other farms. The other two are called North Farm and South Farm and all three stand in a row like this:

Of course they don't look quite like this, but that is because I can't draw very well.

There is a big linden tree between our houses. We can climb along its branches to get from one house to the next.

In the South Farm lives a boy called Olaf – we call him Ollie for short. He has no brothers or sisters so he plays with Lars and Pip. He is eight years old and he can run just as fast as Lars, I think.

In the North Farm there are two girls. I'm so glad that they are not boys too! They are called Britta and Anna. Britta is nine years old and Anna is the same age as me. I think I like them both equally. No, perhaps I like Anna a little better, but only a very little.

There are no other children in the village. It is a very small village: just our three farms, the North Farm, the South Farm and the Middle Farm. And only six children – Lars and Pip and me, Ollie and Britta and Anna.

2. Brothers are a nuisance

Lars and Pip and I used all to sleep in the same room, the right-hand gable room quite close to the attic. Now I have the left-hand gable room to myself, the one that Grandma used to have – but I'll tell you more about that later.

Sometimes it was great fun sleeping in the same room as the boys. But only sometimes. It was fun when we lay and told each other ghost stories in the evening, although it was terrifying too. Lars knew such dreadful ghost stories, that frightened me so much that I had to hide my head under the bed clothes for a long, long time afterwards. Pip never told ghost stories. He only talked about the adventures he was going to have when he grew up. He said he was going to America where there were Red Indians and he would be an Indian Chief.

One evening when Lars had told us a creepy story of a ghost that went about moving all the furniture in the house where he lived, I was so frightened that I really thought I was going to die. It was almost dark in the room and my bed stood far away from Lars' and Pip's. Suddenly a chair began to move backwards and forwards. Of course I thought there was a ghost in our house too, like the one Lars had been telling us about, and that it was going to move all our furniture. I shrieked at the top of my voice.

Then I heard Lars and Pip giggling, and what do you think they had done? They had tied strings on to one of the chairs and were lying in their beds, dragging at it and making it move. That was just like them. At first I was very angry, but then I couldn't help laughing too.

When you sleep in the same room as older brothers, you are never allowed to settle anything for yourself. It was always Lars who decided when to put out the light. When I wanted to read, he always wanted to tell ghost stories in the dark, and if I was sleepy and wanted to go to sleep, Lars and Pip wanted to play games.

Lars had no bedside lamp, so he had tied a long string round the electric switch near the door and jerked it from his bed. He said he was going to be an electrical engineer when he grew up. I don't know exactly what that is, but Lars says it is something very grand. Pip is going to be an Indian Chief, at least he always used to say so, but the other day I heard him say that he was going to be an engine driver.

I don't know what I'm going to be. Perhaps a mother because I like tiny little babies. I have seven dolls for children, but I shall soon be too big to play with dolls. I think it must be dull to be grown up.

My best doll is called Bella. She has blue eyes and black, curly hair. She has a doll's bed with a pink coverlet and pink sheets, but the boys have painted a moustache round her mouth. I'm glad I don't sleep in their room any longer.

Anyone looking out of the window in the boys' room can

look straight into Ollie's. An elm tree grows between our two houses, and once our father and Ollie's father decided that they would cut it down because it kept the sun out of the rooms. But the three boys made such a fuss and begged so hard that the tree might stay, that in the end it was left, and there it stands to this day.

3. My happiest birthday

I think that my birthday and Christmas Eve are the two happiest days in the whole year. I had my happiest birthday when I was seven years old, and this is what happened.

I woke early. I was still sleeping in Lars' and Pip's room, but when I woke Lars and Pip were fast asleep. My bed creaks so I began turning round and round in bed so that the creaking would wake the boys. I could not shout to them, for whoever has a birthday must always stay asleep until they are woken. But they went on sleeping instead of getting up and giving me my birthday tray.

However, I made my bed give a really loud creak, and at last Pip sat up and began to scratch his head. Then he woke Lars and they both crept out of the room and down the stairs. I heard Mother rattling the cups in the kitchen and I could hardly lie still, I was so excited.

At last I heard footsteps on the stairs, so I shut my eyes as tightly as I could. Then – bang – the door opened and there stood Father and Mother and Lars and Pip and Agda, our maid. Mother was carrying my tray and on it I saw a cup of chocolate, a vase of flowers and a big iced cake with 'Lisa 7' on it in sugar icing. Agda had baked it. But I couldn't see any presents and I began to think it was going to be a very odd birthday.

Then Father said: 'Drink your chocolate and after that we'll see if we can find you a present or two.'

Then I knew that I was going to have a big surprise, and I

drank my chocolate very quickly, and Mother tied a handkerchief round my eyes and Father turned me round and round, and then he picked me up and carried me somewhere, but where, of course, I could not see.

I heard Lars and Pip running beside us, and I felt them too, for they kept on pinching my toes and crying: 'Guess where you are now!'

Father took me down the stairs and in and out and once for a moment I felt as if we were out of doors.

Then we went up the stairs again. At last Mother took off the handkerchief, and I saw I was in a room where I thought I had never been before. At least that's what I thought at first, but when I looked out of the window I saw the gable of the North Farm just a little farther away and Britta and Anna standing at the window of their room waving to me.

I realized that I was in Grandma's old room and that Father had gone round and round like that just to confuse me.

Grandma lived with us when I was small but a couple of years ago she had moved to Aunt Frida's. Since then Mother had kept her weaving loom in this room, and there used to be great heaps of rags on the floor with which she made rag mats. But now there was no loom and no rags.

It all looked so lovely that I almost thought a wizard must have been in there. Mother said yes there had been a wizard around and that the wizard was Father, and that he had conjured up a room for me that was to be my very own. This was my birthday present, she said.

I was so pleased that I shouted with joy, and thought it was the best birthday present I could ever have. Father said that Mother had had a hand in making the room. Father had put on the wallpaper – a lovely wallpaper with lots and lots of little bunches of flowers all over it. Mother had made the curtains.

Father had gone down to his carpentry shop in the evenings and made a whole chest of drawers, *and* a round table, *and* a shelf, *and* three chairs, and he had painted them all white. And Mother had made the rag mats that lay on the floor and which had red, yellow and green edges. I had seen her weaving them during the winter but never thought for a moment they were for me. I expect I saw Father making the furniture too, but Father is always making things for people during the winter so I didn't really notice.

Lars and Pip hauled my bed across the attic and into my new room and Lars said: 'We'll come and see you every evening and tell you ghost stories.'

I ran into Lars' and Pip's room to fetch my dolls. I had four small dolls and three large ones, for I had kept all the dolls I had ever been given since I was quite a little girl.

First of all I made room on the shelf for the small dolls. I laid down a bit of red stuff as a rug, and on it I stood my pretty little dolls' furniture which Grandma had given me at Christmas, and then I moved my little dolls' beds there and lastly the

small dolls themselves. Now they had their own room just like me, although it was not their birthday.

I put the large doll's bed in which Bella slept in a corner quite close to my own bed, and the dolls' pram where Hans and Greta slept in another corner. My room looked lovely when all this was done.

After that I ran into Lars' and Pip's room and fetched all my boxes and other things that I had kept in the boys' chest of drawers.

Pip said: 'Fine! Now I shall have more room for my birds' eggs!'

I had thirteen books of my own and I stood them up on the shelf too, and all my boxes of bookmarks. I had so many bookmarks. We swapped them at school. But my twenty *special* bookmarks I wouldn't swap with anyone. My best one was a large angel with a pink dress and wings.

I found a place for everything on my shelf. It was wonderful to have a room of my very own.

4. Turnips and a kitten

I got a lot of money in my savings box later on because I helped to thin out the turnips. All we Bullerby children used to help. Originally Lars and Pip and I only helped with the turnips belonging to the Middle Farm, and Britta and Anna with those belonging to the North Farm, and Ollie those belonging to the South Farm. But instead of that we now all worked together. We were paid for every row we thinned – so much for the long rows and less for the shorter ones.

We wore aprons made of sacks so that we should not hurt our knees when we knelt on the ground. Britta and Anna and I tied scarves round our heads so that Mother said we looked like little old women.

We had an enamel pail of lemonade with us in case we should feel thirsty. Funnily enough we were all thirsty at the same time, so we cut long straws, put one end into the pail and knelt on the ground round it and drank.

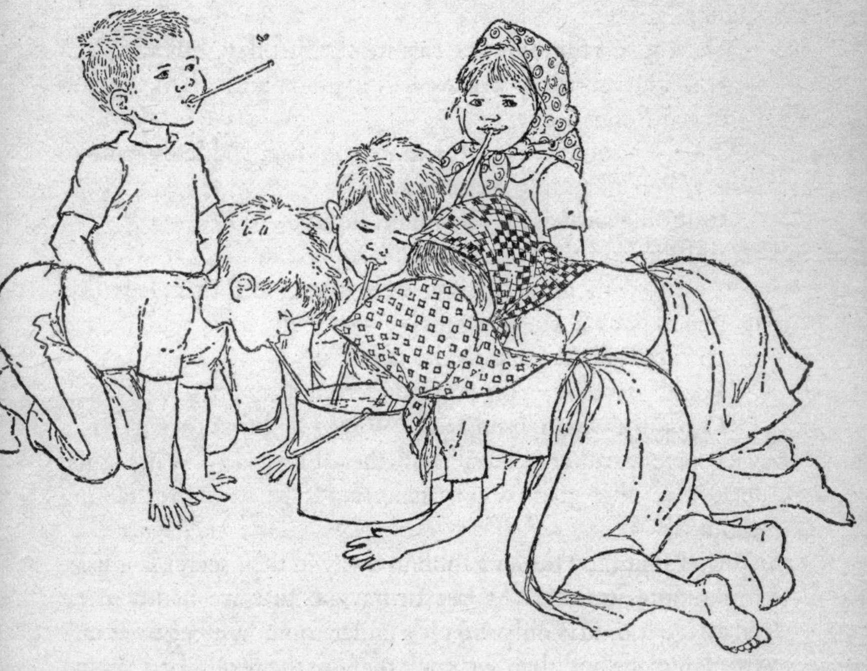

It was fun drinking lemonade through a straw and we drank and drank until suddenly there was no lemonade left. Then Lars took the pail and ran to the well in the orchard close by and drew water for us, and we drank the water. It was just as much fun, but not nearly so good.

Finally, Ollie lay down flat on his back on the ground and said: 'Listen how my tummy goes cluck, cluck.'

He had so much water in his tummy that we all went over and listened to it going cluck, cluck, whenever he moved.

We talked all the time while we were thinning out the turnips and told each other stories. Lars tried to tell us ghost stories, but ghost stories aren't frightening when the sun is shining.

We enjoyed thinning the turnips the first day, but after that it grew a little boring. But we had to go on until all the turnips had been thinned out.

One day soon after we had begun Lars suddenly said to Ollie: 'Petruska saldo bumbum.'

And Ollie answered: 'Kolifink, kolifink.'

And Pip said: 'Mojsi dojsi fillibom ararat.'

We asked them what they were saying and then Lars told us that it was a secret language that only boys understood, much too difficult for girls, he said.

'Pooh,' we said, 'you don't understand it yourselves!'

'Certainly we do,' said Lars. 'What I said first meant: "It is very nice weather today," and then Pip said: "What good luck that the girls don't understand what we're talking about."'

After that they began gabbling away in their secret language for minutes on end. At last Britta said that we had a secret language too, that only we girls understood. We began to talk that language and then we knelt there in the turnip bed talking our different languages the whole morning. I myself could not hear any difference in the language, but Lars said that our language wasn't a language at all. The boys' language was much better, he said, for it was almost Russian.

'Kolifink, kolifink,' said Ollie again and we had learnt so much of the boys' language that we knew that this meant, 'Certainly, certainly.'

From then on Britta and Anna and I never called Ollie anything but 'Ollie Kolifink'.

One afternoon when we were thinning turnips and had just sat down on a pile of sacks to drink our chocolate and eat our sandwiches, the sky suddenly grew quite black and there was a frightful thunderstorm. It hailed too. It hailed so much that it lay in drifts just as if it had snowed.

'We'll run to Kristina's cottage,' said Lars. We almost always do what Lars tells us, so we all ran to Kristina's little red cottage which wasn't far away. Luckily Kristina was at home. She is

an old woman who looks very much like Grandma and is very kind. I have visited her many, many times.

'Oh dear,' she said, raising her hands in dismay. 'You poor wet children.'

She made up a big fire in the open stove and told us to take off all our wet clothes and warm our feet in front of it. And then she made waffles for us in a waffle pan over the fire, and coffee in a coffee pot that stood on three legs in the middle of the fire.

Kristina has three cats and one of them had just had kittens. They lay in a basket and mewed and were dear little things. There were four of them and Kristina said that she had to give them all away except one because otherwise the house would be over-run by cats and there would be no room left for her.

'Oh, can't we have them?' cried Anna.

Kristina said yes, of course we could, but she wasn't at all sure if our mothers would be very pleased if we suddenly arrived home with the three kittens.

'Everybody likes kittens,' said Britta.

And we begged and begged her that we might take them – on approval anyway. There were just enough kittens to go round. One for the North Farm, one for the Middle Farm and one for the South Farm. Lars chose the one for us. It was a little tabby with a white spot on its forehead. Britta and Anna chose the one that was quite white, and Ollie had the black one.

When our clothes were dry we went home with our kittens. I was so glad that the mother cat had one left – otherwise she would have no children at all.

We called our kitten Murray. Britta and Anna called theirs Sammy and Ollie called his Malcolm. None of our mothers objected to our having the kittens so we were allowed to keep them.

I played with Murray a great deal. I fastened a scrunched up piece of paper on to a string and ran round and round with it, and Murray ran after me and tried to catch the paper. Lars and Pip also played with him to begin with, but they soon tired, so it was I who had to look after him and give him his food.

He drank milk from a saucer in the kitchen. He did not drink as people drink: he stuck out his little pink tongue, and then lapped up the milk.

I arranged a basket for him to sleep in, and made it very soft and comfortable. Sometimes we let Murray, Sammy and Malcolm play together on the lawn, for after all they were brothers, and so of course they wanted to see each other.

I earned nine shillings by my turnip-thinning and put everything into my savings box for I was saving up for a red bicycle.

5. How Ollie got his dog

Ollie has no brothers or sisters, but he has a dog – and Malcolm too, of course. His dog is called Svipp. I'll tell you how Ollie got Svipp exactly as he told the story to us.

Between Bullerby and the big village there lived a cobbler called Mr Good. He was *called* Good but he was not good, not in any way whatsoever. He never had our shoes ready when we went to fetch them, even if he had promised them by then again and again.

Svipp was his dog to begin with, but he was never kind to him. So of course Svipp was the most bad-tempered dog in the neighbourhood. He was almost always tied up in his kennel, and whenever anybody came to see Mr Good Svipp used to rush out at them and bark.

We were all terrified of him, and never dared go anywhere near him. We were afraid of Mr Good too, for he was always so cross and used to say 'Children are all little nuisances and ought to be beaten every day.' Svipp was beaten jolly often, although he was a dog and not a child. Perhaps Mr Good thought that dogs should be beaten every day too. And when Mr Good drank too much beer he always forgot to feed Svipp.

When Svipp was Mr Good's dog, I thought he was a bad, ugly dog. He was so dirty and untidy, and he growled and barked and snapped all the time. Now I think he is a nice, good-looking dog, and it is Ollie who has made him so, just because Ollie is so good and kind himself. This is what happened.

One day when Ollie took his shoes to the cobbler and Svipp rushed out of his kennel as usual barking and looking very fierce, Ollie stopped and talked to him. He called him 'good dog' and told him he must not bark like that. Ollie stood a little way off while he was talking, of course, so that Svipp could not get at him. Svipp looked as furious as ever and did not behave like a 'good dog' at all.

When Ollie went to fetch his shoes he brought a nice bone for Svipp. Svipp barked and growled, but he was so hungry that he began gnawing the bone at once. While he was eating Ollie still stood a little way off and again told Svipp what a good dog he was.

Ollie had to go and ask for those shoes of his quite a lot of times before they were ready, and he always took something nice for Svipp to eat. And would you believe it, there came a day when Svipp no longer growled at Ollie, but only barked in the way that dogs do when they see someone they like. And then Ollie went up close to Svipp and Svipp licked his hands.

Then one day the shoemaker fell and broke his leg. He did not care whether Svipp had any food or not, but Ollie did. He went to see Mr Good and asked whether he might look after Svipp until Mr Good's leg was better. How he dared, I don't know! But Mr Good said: 'He'll fly at your throat if you go anywhere near him – you see if he doesn't!'

Ollie went out to Svipp and patted him, and the shoemaker watched through the window. So he said that Ollie might look after Svipp until he could get about again himself.

Ollie tidied up Svipp's kennel and gave him new straw and cleaned out his water bowl, filling it with fresh water, and of course he gave him plenty of food. He began to take him for walks on his lead, and even brought him all the way to Bullerby.

Svipp jumped about and barked with delight, for he had been tied up for so long that he was dead sick of it.

Every day while Mr Good's leg was bad Ollie fetched Svipp and took him for a run. We all ran with them too, but Svipp

liked Ollie best and if anyone else held his lead he began to growl.

But as soon as the cobbler was well again he said to Ollie: 'That's enough of all this nonsense. The dog was bought to be a watchdog, and a watchdog he's got to be. He'll stay in his kennel, so that's that.'

Svipp thought he was going for a walk as usual, and he

jumped about and barked noisily whenever he saw Ollie. But when Ollie had to go off without him he whined and yelped and Ollie said he sounded very unhappy. Ollie himself was miserable for a long time, till at last his father went off to Mr Good and succeeded in buying Svipp for Ollie.

All we Bullerby children watched Ollie bath Svipp in one of the outhouses. He let us help him. When Svipp had been bathed and dried and combed he looked exactly like any other dog.

He slept every night under Ollie's bed, and when we came home from school Svipp ran to meet Ollie and carried his satchel for him. But he never came as far as Mr Good's cottage. Perhaps he was afraid Mr Good would come out and catch him again.

6. Grandpa

It's fun having an animal of your very own. I should like to have a dog too, but I haven't. We have so many animals in Bullerby: horses and cows and calves and pigs and sheep. And Mother has such a lot of hens that our house is called Bullerby's hennery – that's what people call it. Mother sends eggs and tiny chicks away all over the country.

None of these animals is really mine, like Svipp is Ollie's, but I have rabbits that are properly mine. They live in a hutch that my father made for me, and I have to go and give them grass and dandelion leaves every day. In winter I move the hutch into the barn.

My rabbits have lots of babies. I have sold a good many to Ollie. Pip had a rabbit of his own once but he got tired of it just as he gets tired of everything except his birds' eggs.

There is an old tree in our garden that we call the 'owl tree' because owls live in it. One day Pip climbed up into the owl tree and took an egg from the owl's nest. There were four eggs so that the owl had three eggs left. Pip blew the egg and put it in the drawer with the rest of his collection. Then he suddenly thought he would play a joke on the mother owl, so he climbed up again and put a hen's egg in the nest in place of the egg he had taken.

The mother owl never noticed the difference. She went on sitting on the eggs, and then one fine day there were three small owls and a chick in the nest.

How astonished the mother owl must have been to see that one of her young ones was a little yellow ball of fluff!

Pip was afraid that the owl might be unkind to the chick so he took it away.

'And anyhow it's my chick!' he said.

He tied a red ribbon round one of its legs so that he might recognize it and let it loose among mother's chickens. He called it Albert, but when Albert grew a little larger he turned out to be a little hen and not a cock. Then Pip called it Albertina, and now Albertina is a big hen and whenever Pip eats an egg he says: 'I expect Albertina laid this egg for me!'

Albertina flies about and flaps her wings more than any of the other hens. Pip says that it is probably because she was born in an owl's nest, and thinks she can fly.

At one time Lars thought that he also would like to have some animals of his own. So he set three vole-traps in the pighouse and caught sixteen big voles which he shut up in a barrel. Then he painted a large poster which said 'Bullerby's Vole House' and fastened it to the barrel. But in the night all the voles escaped, so that was the end of the vole house.

'What did you want a vole house for anyway?' asked Britta. 'Voles don't lay eggs.'

'I just thought it would be fun to have a vole house,' said Lars crossly. He was annoyed because the voles had got away.

Britta and Anna had no dog and no rabbits nor any other farm animals of their own – but they had a grandfather. He was the kindest grandfather in the whole world, I am certain of that. All we children called him Grandpa, although he was not our grandfather really: he was only Britta and Anna's grandfather. He lived in a room at the top of the North Farm. It was a nice room and he was such a kind grandfather that we all loved to go up there when we had nothing else to do.

Grandpa always sat in a rocking chair and had a long white beard exactly like Father Christmas. He had very bad eyesight so that he saw almost nothing. He could not read any books or papers, but that did not matter for he knew everything that had been written in books.

He told us stories from the Bible and what the world was like when he was a little boy.

Britta and Anna and I read the paper to him, and told him who had died and who were having their fiftieth birthdays and all the accidents and announcements in the paper. If the paper said that a thunderbolt had fallen anywhere, then Grandpa could tell us at least twenty other places that had been struck by lightning in olden days. And if we read that someone had been chased by a bull, then Grandpa told us about all the other people he had known who had been chased by angry bulls.

So it always took quite a long time to read the paper to Grandpa. Sometimes the boys read to him, but he liked Britta and Anna and me best for the boys read so carelessly and skipped a lot of births, deaths and marriages and things of that sort.

Grandpa kept a box of tools in his cupboard and he let the boys borrow tools from him. He also helped them to carve boats and other things, although he could not see. And when

the boys wanted to make tin soldiers, they went to Grandpa and heated the lead on his stove.

Grandpa always had a box of apples in his cupboard, I don't mean always of course, but when apples were in season, and whenever we went up to him he used to give us each an apple. We bought him cough lozenges when we went into the village, and he had a bag of them in the corner cupboard in his room.

So we got both apples and cough lozenges from him.

Grandpa had pots of begonias in his window and he looked after them very well although he was almost blind. He would often talk to them for quite a long time. He also had some lovely pictures on the walls in his room. Two of them I specially liked. One was of Jonah in the whale's belly, and the other of a serpent which had escaped from a zoo, and was just squeezing a man to death. Well, perhaps they weren't exactly pretty pictures, but they were exciting.

When the weather was good Grandpa used to go out for a walk. He had a stick to feel his way and in summer time he generally sat under the large tree that grew just outside the North Farm. As he sat there in the sunshine he would suddenly say: 'Well, well!'

We asked him why he said 'Well, well!' and he told us that it was because he was thinking of the days when he was young. That must have been a very, very long time ago, I suppose.

But how nice it is that we have such a kind Grandpa! I like him so much that I would rather have him than a dog.

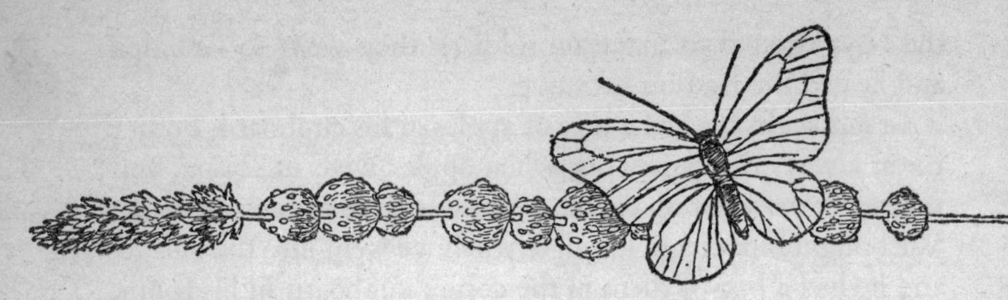

7. We sleep in the barn

One day Pip said to me: 'Tonight Lars and I are going to sleep in the barn on top of the hay, and Ollie too, if he's allowed.'

'Only tramps sleep in the hay,' said I.

'No, they don't,' said Pip. 'We've asked Mother and she says we may.'

I ran off and told Britta and Anna.

'Then we'll sleep in *our* barn,' they said, 'and you too, Lisa.'

So that was settled. What fun it was going to be. It was only annoying that it was the boys who had thought of it first and not us. I immediately ran home to Mother and asked if I might. Mother did not think that little girls should sleep in barns, but I said that if boys were allowed to enjoy themselves, why couldn't little girls too? Then she gave in.

We could scarcely wait till the evening. Lars said: 'Are you girls going to sleep in the hay too? You daren't! What if there are ghosts!'

'Of course we dare,' we said, and we made ourselves sandwiches to take with us in case we were hungry in the night.

When the boys saw us doing it they made themselves sandwiches too.

At eight o'clock we went to the barn. The boys were going to sleep in the Middle Farm barn and we in the one belonging to the North Farm. Each of us had taken a horse blanket and Ollie took Svipp with him. Lucky Ollie to have a dog!

'Good night, little tramps,' said Father, and Mother added: 'I suppose you'll come in tomorrow morning and buy milk. All tramps do that.'

When we said good night to the boys Lars said: 'Sleep well! If you can! Last year we found an adder in the hay in the North Farm barn. I wonder if there are any there this year.'

And Pip added: 'Perhaps there are and perhaps there are not! But there will certainly be lots of little field mice. You'll hate that!'

'Poor children,' we said to the boys, 'are you afraid of field mice? If so you had better go home and sleep in your own beds.'

Then we went off with our blankets and our sandwiches. It was quite light out of doors but it was almost dark in the barn.

'Bags to sleep in the middle,' I cried.

And then we settled ourselves down in the hay. It smelt so good but it was very prickly, but when we had rolled ourselves up in our blankets we were really very comfortable.

We lay there talking and wondering what it would be like to be real tramps who always slept in barns. Anna said she thought it would be nice. We were not in the least sleepy, only hungry, so we ate our sandwiches before it grew too dark.

Soon it was so dark round us that when we held up a hand in front of our faces we could not see it. I was glad I was in the middle between Britta and Anna.

The hay was rustling in a very strange way. Britta and Anna both wriggled closer to me.

'What if a real tramp came to sleep here tonight?' whispered Britta. 'You know – without asking if he might.'

We lay quite silent and thought about that for a moment, and then, suddenly, we heard a most bloodcurdling yell. It sounded as if thousands of ghosts were howling at the same time. It was amazing that all of us did not die of fright then and there.

But we didn't, but oh how we shrieked, and how Lars and Pip and Ollie laughed! For it was the boys who had yelled, and made all that rustling in the hay as they came creeping towards us.

Britta said that it was very dangerous to be frightened like that because the blood might go solid in one's veins, and she said that she would tell her mother about it.

'Oh it was only a joke!' said Lars.

And Pip chanted: 'Tell-tale-tit. Tell-tale-tit!'

Anna cried out that she felt as if the blood had already gone a little solid in her veins. But we soon got over our fright.

At last the boys went back to their own barn and we began to wonder whether we would slip over and try to frighten them too, but we were so sleepy that we decided not to.

We were woken by the North Farm cock and also because we felt so cold. Oh how cold it was! We were all shivering.

We did not know what time it was but we thought that it might be about time to get up. Just as we stuck our noses

outside the barn doors Lars and Pip and Ollie came out from the Middle Farm barn. They were shivering with cold too.

We all ran into our kitchen to warm ourselves up, and, would you believe it, it was so early that no one was awake, for it was only half past four. But Agda's alarm clock soon went off as she had to get up to milk the cows, and she gave us all warm milk and buns. How good they tasted!

Afterwards I went upstairs and crept into my own bed, for I felt that I wanted to sleep a little more. It must have been a very wise person who invented beds, for actually you sleep much better in your own bed than in the hay.

8. Anna and I decide to run away

There was no one with whom I enjoyed playing more than with Anna. We had a great many pretence games that only she and I knew about. Sometimes we pretended that we were two ladies visiting each other. Then Anna called herself Mrs Benson and I called myself Mrs Larson. Anna looked very grand when she was Mrs Benson and she spoke in a genteel voice. I spoke that way too when I was Mrs Larson.

Sometimes we pretended that Mrs Benson and Mrs Larson quarrelled and then Anna would say: 'Mrs Larson, you'd better take your horrid children home!' She meant my dolls of course.

Then I would answer: 'Well, I never, Mrs Benson, it's *your* children who are so horrid!'

We were soon friends again, and pretended we were going shopping to buy satin and velvet and sweets. We had pretend money which we had made ourselves when we were up with Grandpa. We were always afraid that Lars and the others would hear us when we were pretending, for of course they would only laugh at us. It did not matter if Grandpa heard us because he pretended a lot himself sometimes, and we bought things from him with our pretend money.

Anna and I often sat up with Grandpa when it was raining and read the paper to him. When Grandpa was a little boy both his father and his mother had died and he had to live with other people who were not at all kind to him. He had to work very hard although he was so small, and he was often beaten and

given very little food, so at last he grew tired of it all and ran away. And you would never believe how many exciting adventures he had before he at last found some kind people where he could stay for good.

One rainy day when Anna and I were sitting with Grandpa and had finished reading the paper Anna said: 'Grandpa, tell us about when you ran away.'

'Oh dear, oh dear,' said Grandpa, 'you've heard it so often.'

But we begged and begged him to tell us again until at last

he did. Afterwards Anna said: 'It must be fun to run away. I feel rather like doing so myself.'

'Yes, but first you must have some unkind people to run away from,' I said.

'That's not at all necessary,' said Anna. 'You can run away from anything. Just for a bit! And then come home again.'

'Well, let's do it,' said I.

'What do you say to that, Grandpa?' said Anna. 'Do you think we can do it?'

And Grandpa said certainly, there was no harm in running away for just a little while. So we decided to do so. It had to happen at night, of course. And no one must know. We told Grandpa he mustn't tell anyone. He promised that he would not.

I always found it very hard to keep awake in the evenings, so I couldn't imagine what I could do to keep awake until it was time to run away.

'You can go to sleep!' said Anna. 'We'll tie a piece of string on to your big toe and hang it out of your window and then I'll come and pull it and wake you up.'

Anna said she would pick a lot of branches and twigs and put them in her bed, and she thought that would keep her awake until all the others had gone to sleep because she would be so uncomfortable.

Then we asked Grandpa what we ought to take with us when we ran away, and he said that we had better take a little food and perhaps a little money if we had any. We thought we would run away that very night so we were kept busy getting everything ready.

I went to Mother and asked if I might have a few sandwiches and she said: 'What's this, are you hungry already? You've only just had dinner.'

I could not, of course, tell her why I wanted the sandwiches, so I just said nothing. Then I took a few shillings from the money I had earned by turnip-thinning and put it under my pillow. Then off I went to find a long string to tie round my big toe.

In the evening we all played rounders and when at last it was time to go to bed Anna and I winked at one another and whispered: 'Half past ten!'

I hugged Father and Mother very hard when I said good night for I thought that now I would not see them for quite a long time. And when Mother said: 'Tomorrow you and I must pick red currants,' I was very sorry for Mother because of course tomorrow she would not have a little girl to help her.

I went up to my room and tied the string round my big toe and threw the end of it out of the window. Then I went to bed as I wanted to get to sleep so that I should not be tired when it came to running away.

Generally I went to sleep as soon as I put my head on the pillow, but that night I just could not get off. I tried my hardest, but whenever I turned in my bed the string strained round my big toe, and I began to think of what Mother would say when she came next morning and saw that my bed was empty. I felt so sorry for her that I began to cry and I cried for a very, very long time.

Suddenly I woke up. My big toe felt odd and I could not understand what it was, but then I remembered. Someone was pulling the string.

'All right, Anna, I'm coming,' I cried, and jumped out of bed and ran to the window. It was full daylight and there stood Lars below my window pulling at the string. I was furiously angry.

'Oh, oh,' I shouted, 'stop that!'

'Why?' asked Lars.

'Because the string is tied to my big toe,' I screamed.

Lars laughed and laughed and then he said: 'There was a funnier fish on that line than I expected!'

Then he wanted to know why I had tied the string on to my big toe but I didn't stop to tell him that. I ran straight to the North Farm wondering whether Anna had perhaps gone off by herself. Britta was sitting on the steps playing with the kitten.

'Where's Anna?' I asked.

'Asleep,' answered Britta.

I went up to the girls' room and there lay Anna – snoring.

I tried to tie the string round her big toe but she woke up.

'Oh,' she said. 'What's the time?'

When I told her that it was eight o'clock in the morning she was absolutely silent for a long time.

Then she said: 'People who say they can't sleep at night should try lying on lots of twigs and branches. You can't imagine how sleepy they make you.'

Then we went up to Grandpa to read the paper to him. When we came rushing in to his room he looked up in surprise and asked: 'What's this! Haven't you run away after all?'

'Another time,' we answered.

9. The great storm

Shall I tell you about the great storm which came just before Christmas? It was the worst storm Father could remember, he said.

Every day from the beginning of December as we set off for school Lars used to say: 'There'll be no snow at Christmas this year, you'll see.'

It made me sad every time he said it, as I was longing for a white Christmas, but day after day passed, and not the least little snowflake came floating down. But in Christmas week itself, as we sat in school doing arithmetic, Pip suddenly cried: 'Look! It's snowing!'

And it was. We were so pleased we all began shouting, and teacher told us to stand up and sing a song we knew called 'Now has winter come indeed'.

When we went out into the school yard at break there was a thin, white covering of snow. We trampled out a large figure of eight in the snow, and ran round and round it shouting: 'Hurrah, hurrah,' but Lars said: 'This is all the snow there'll be.'

When we went to school next day, however, there was so

much snow that we had to plough our way through it, and it was still snowing. But Lars said: 'This is the last of the snow, and there'll be plenty of time for it to melt before Christmas Day.'

But he was absolutely wrong. When we reached the school it began to snow more than ever. It snowed so hard that it was quite white outside the window, and it was impossible to see even across the school yard. It went on the whole day and then it began to blow too.

It blew and snowed, and snowed and blew till at last our teacher grew anxious and said: 'I don't know how you Bullerby children are going to get home today.'

She asked us whether we would like to stay the night with her, and we should have liked to do so very much indeed, but we knew that they would all be anxious at home if we did not come. So we said we had better go. She sent us home at once before it grew dark.

It was one o'clock when we left school, and oh what deep snow drifts there were already! *And* how it blew! We had to walk almost bent double.

'Have you had enough snow now?' cried Britta angrily to Lars.

'It isn't Christmas yet,' said Lars, but we could scarcely hear what he said because of the wind.

We walked and walked and walked. We held hands so that we should not lose each other. The snow was high above my knees and when it is like that it is difficult to walk quickly. The wind blew right through us until we were so frozen that we had no feeling in our toes and fingers and noses.

Finally my legs were so tired that I told Lars I wanted to rest for a moment.

'Not on your life,' said Lars.

Anna was tired too and wanted to rest, but Lars said it was dangerous. Then Anna and I began to cry for we thought we should never get home to Bullerby again.

We had only got halfway when suddenly Ollie said: 'We'll go in to the cobbler's! He can't eat us.'

Anna and I wanted to go in to the cobbler's even if he did eat us.

It was blowing so hard that we were almost blown in through the cobbler's door. He was not very pleased to see us.

'What are you kids doing out in this sort of weather?' he asked.

We did not dare to reply that it had not been 'this sort of weather' when we left home. We took off our coats and sat down and looked at him while he went on mending shoes. We were very hungry but we did not dare to say so.

The cobbler made coffee for himself and drank it and ate sandwiches, but he did not offer us anything. It was very different from when we went to Kristina's cottage in a thunderstorm.

At dusk it stopped snowing and blowing, but there were such large drifts that we could not imagine how we were going to get home. I longed to be at home with Mother and comfortably in bed.

Suddenly we heard sleigh bells out in the snow. We rushed to the window and looked out, and there was Father with the snow plough. We opened the door and shrieked at him, although the cobbler said crossly: 'Don't let the cold air in!'

Father was very pleased when he saw us, and shouted that he just had to plough as far as the village, but that he would pick us up on his way back. And so he did, and Anna and I were allowed to sit in the snow plough but the others had to walk behind it. The plough had cleared the road so well that there were no more difficulties where it had passed.

When we got home Mother was standing at the kitchen window looking out anxiously. Lars and Pip and I were given hot meat soup with dumplings in it, and I really don't think I have ever tasted anything so good either before or since. I ate three platefuls. Afterwards I went to bed at once and that was lovely.

Mother said that she had had a strong feeling that Father should take the snow plough, for she was certain we were somewhere on the road. It was lucky that she had had that feeling for otherwise we should probably have had to stay the whole night with the cobbler.

10. It will soon be Christmas

The next day the sun shone and the snow lay white and beautiful on all the trees and it was the last day of school before Christmas. Our teacher said she had not slept the whole night, wondering how we had got on in the snow.

As it was the last day before Christmas she read us the Christmas story. Everything felt different and just before we started home the best thing of all happened.

Teacher had written to Stockholm and had ordered story books for us all. Earlier in the term she had shown us a large sheet on which were some pretty pictures out of various story books. She told us to choose which books we wanted to buy.

I had ordered two, and Lars and Pip two each also. There were lovely princes and princesses on the cover of mine. And the books arrived just on this last day of school. Teacher went round dividing them out. I could scarcely wait until she gave me mine, but Mother had said we must not read them until Christmas Eve.

Before we went home we sang all the carols we knew and teacher said she hoped we should have a happy Christmas. I, at any rate, was quite sure we should.

Britta and Anna and I ran to the village shop and bought red and yellow, green, white and blue shiny paper to make baskets to hang on the Christmas tree. Then we went home. The snow made the forest light and sparkling.

Suddenly, as we were walking along, Britta took out her

story book and smelt it. Then we all smelt it too. New books smell so good that you can almost feel from the smell how lovely it will be to read them.

Then Britta began to read her book aloud. Her mother also had told her that the books were to be kept till Christmas Eve, but Britta said she was only going to read a little tiny bit. When she had read her little bit we all thought it so exciting that we begged her to go on. Then she read a little bit more, but that was no good for when she had finished that little bit it was just as exciting.

'I must know whether the prince was bewitched or not,' said Lars.

So then she had to read a little bit more. She went on like that and by the time we had at last reached home Britta had read the whole book to us. She said it did not matter because she would read it all over again on Christmas Eve.

When we got home Mother and Agda were just making the Christmas sausage, and the whole house had been cleaned and polished and looked lovely. As soon as we had eaten our tea we went out and Lars and Pip and I built a large and splendid snow lantern in the garden. Britta, Anna and Ollie came and helped.

There were a whole lot of sparrows and bullfinches and tits in the lime trees and they looked so hungry that I ran in and asked whether we might not put up the Christmas sheaf a little earlier than usual, and Father said yes. So we all went down to the barn and fetched five sheaves of wheat that had been carefully kept for Christmas when the threshing was done.

We put them up in the apple tree in our garden and it was not long before the birds were there enjoying them. I expect they thought that it was Christmas Eve already. It all looked lovely with the Christmas sheaves and snow and everything.

In the evening Britta, Anna and I went and sat with Grandpa and made baskets for the Christmas tree from the coloured paper. The boys were there too. First of all they would not help us with the Christmas baskets, but after a time they couldn't resist joining in.

We all sat round Grandpa's round table, and we made fifty-four baskets, which we divided into three so that there were

eighteen baskets for the North Farm, eighteen for the Middle Farm and eighteen for the South Farm.

Grandpa gave us apples and sweets. While we were sitting there I kept on thinking that next day we should be baking gingerbreads. It was all almost as much fun as Christmas Eve itself.

In the middle of everything Lars ran out into the garden and lit the candle in the snow lantern. It looked wonderful shining in the darkness.

'Poor Grandpa, you can't see the snow lantern,' said Anna. 'Shall we sing to you instead?' she asked – for Grandpa liked to hear us sing. So we sang the carols we had learnt at school.

'Don't you think that Christmas is fun?' whispered Anna to me afterwards. And I said that I thought it was the greatest fun I knew. All we Bullerby children always have such a good time then. We have a great deal of fun at other times too, of course, in the summer and in the winter, in the spring and in the autumn. In fact, we have a happy time all the year round, but Christmas is best of all.

11. Christmas in Bullerby

I don't know when Christmas starts in other places, but in Bullerby it starts the day we bake ginger snaps. We have almost as much fun that day as on Christmas Eve. Lars and Pip and I each get a big chunk of ginger-snap dough, and we can bake it in the shape of anything we want. The last time we were to bake ginger snaps, Lars forgot all about it and went to the forest with Father to get wood. Right in the middle of the forest he remembered what day it was and rushed home so fast that the snow whirled round him, Father said.

Pip and I had already started to bake. It was just as well that Lars came a little late because the best ginger snap mould we have is a pig, and when Lars is there it's almost impossible for Pip and me to get it. But this time we had baked ten pigs each before Lars came puffing home from the forest. How he hurried to catch up with us!

When we had almost finished baking we put all our last little pieces of dough together and made a big prize biscuit. We always do this. Then in the afternoon, when all the ginger snaps had come out of the oven, we put 332 dried peas in a bottle and went all round Bullerby to let everyone guess how many peas there were. The one who made the closest guess would get the big biscuit for a prize.

Lars carried the bottle, Pip carried the prize biscuit, and I carried a notebook where I wrote down everyone's guess. Grandpa was the one who won the prize, and I was so glad. He guessed that there were 320 peas in the bottle, which was

very close. Anna guessed that there were three *thousand* peas. Wasn't that crazy?

The day after we baked the ginger snaps was fun too, for then we went to the forest to cut the Christmas trees. All the fathers go along when we cut the Christmas trees – and all the children too, of course. The mothers have to stay at home and cook, poor things! We took our big sleigh, which we use for carrying the milk from Bullerby to the dairy in the big village. Lars and Pip and I and Britta and Anna and Olaf rode in the sleigh. My daddy walked beside it and drove the horse. Olaf's and Britta's and Anna's daddies walked behind it and laughed and talked. All of us in the sleigh laughed and talked too.

There was so much snow in the forest that we had to shake it out of the fir trees to see if they were pretty or not. We cut three big fir trees, one for each farm. And then we cut a tiny little tree for Grandpa to have in his room, and another little one to give to Kristina, because she is an old woman who lives all alone in her red cottage in the woods.

The night before Christmas Eve I felt sad because I didn't think Mother and Agda could ever get everything ready for Christmas. It looked so untidy all over the house, and especially in the kitchen. I cried a little after I had gone to bed.

On Christmas Eve morning I woke up early and ran down to the kitchen in my nightie to see if it was still untidy. But instead it was beautiful! There were new rag carpets on the floor; there was red and green and white curled tissue paper round the iron pole by the stove; there was a Christmas cloth on the big folding table; and all the copper kettles were polished. I was so happy that I gave Mother a big hug. Lars and Pip came rushing in right after me, and Lars said that even his stomach felt Christmassy when he saw the rag carpets.

On Christmas Eve morning all of us Bullerby children

always go to Kristina's with a basket full of goodies from our mothers. But first we go to Grandpa to wish him a Merry Christmas and watch Britta and Anna decorate his little tree. We help a little too, although Britta and Anna prefer to do it by themselves. Of course Grandpa can't see what we hang on the tree, because he is nearly blind, but when we tell him about it he says that he can see it inside his head.

When we walked over to Kristina's cottage the weather was very beautiful, just as it should be on Christmas Eve. The road that goes to Kristina's cottage is so narrow that we could hardly see it under all the snow. Lars carried the basket, and Pip and Olaf the little fir tree. The boys wouldn't let Britta and Anna and me carry anything. How surprised Kristina was when we came! Well, she probably was just pretending to be surprised, because she knows that we come every year. Lars unpacked everything in the basket and put it on the table, and Kristina just shook her head and said, 'My, my, it's too much, it's much too much!'

I didn't think that it was too much, but it was a lot: a large piece of ham, a sausage, a round cheese, coffee, ginger snaps, candles, sweets, and I don't remember what else. We put the candles on Kristina's tree and danced round it a little while to practise for later on that night. Kristina was very happy, and she stood in the doorway and waved to us as we left.

When we got home Lars and Pip and I decorated our tree. Father helped us. We got the red apples that we were going to use on the tree out of the attic, and then we hung some of our ginger snaps on it. We put raisins and nuts in the Christmas baskets we had made of coloured paper. We also hung up the cotton angels that Mother had used on her tree when she was little – and then, of course, a lot of flags and candles and sweets. The tree looked very pretty when it was finished!

Then it was time to 'dip in the pot'. Mother gave us large slices of rye bread that Agda had baked, and we dipped them in the broth that the ham had cooked in. It was very good. Then there was nothing to do but WAIT. Lars said that times like those hours in the afternoon of Christmas Eve, when you don't do anything but wait and wait, are the kind of things people get grey hairs from. We waited and waited and waited, and from time to time I went to the mirror to see if I had any grey hairs yet. But strangely enough, my hair was just as yellow as ever. Pip hit the clock now and then, because he thought that it had stopped.

When it got dark, it was time at last to take our presents over to North Farm and South Farm. You can't do that when it's light because it wouldn't be exciting at all. Lars and Pip and I put on our red Santa Claus caps and Lars took the Santa Claus mask that he was going to wear later in the evening. (It's Lars who is Santa Claus at our house nowadays. When I was little I thought that there was a real Santa Claus, but I don't think so any more.) Then we took our packages and slipped out into the dark. The sky was full of stars. I looked towards the forest, standing so dark and still, and imagined that perhaps there was a real Santa Claus living there who soon would come, pulling

a sled loaded with Christmas presents. I almost wished that it were true.

There was no light in the kitchen at North Farm. We pounded on the back door, and then we opened it and threw our Christmas packages inside. Britta and Anna came rushing out and said that we had to come in and taste their Christmas cakes and sweets. So we did, and they gave us Christmas packages too. Britta and Anna put on their Santa Claus masks, and we all went over to South Farm to see Olaf. He was sitting in their kitchen, and he was just waiting too. Svipp, his dog, barked like anything when he saw five Santa Clauses coming. Then Olaf put on a mask too, and we all ran out and played Santa Claus in the dark.

At last it was really Christmas Eve, and we ate supper at the folding table in the kitchen. There were candles on the table and an awful lot of food, but I didn't eat much except ham. I did eat porridge, of course, in case I should get the almond. The one who gets the almond in the porridge is sure to get married during the coming year. But I didn't get it. It had broken in two, and Oscar the hired man and Agda each got a piece. How Lars and Pip and I laughed. Agda got cross and said the whole thing was probably one of our tricks. But how could we help it that the almond had broken in two?

We made up rhymes to the porridge too. Lars made up this one:

> You saw the almond break in two,
> So Oscar is certain to marry you.

We thought that was pretty good, but Agda didn't think so. She got a little more cheerful afterwards, when we all helped her to dry the dishes. We did that so that we could get ready sooner and start giving out the presents.

When we finished we went into the dining room. The tree was lighted and so were the candles on the table. I got goose flesh the way I always do when anything's very beautiful and exciting. Father read to us from the Bible about the Christ Child. I read some terribly pretty verses that start this way: 'Oh, little Lord Jesus, asleep in the hay.' It goes on to say in those verses that the Christ Child should really have a whole lot of Christmas presents and a cake. That's what I think too. But instead we're the ones who get all the presents.

While the rest of us sang 'Silent Night', Lars slipped out and in a little while he came back, dressed as Santa Claus, with a big sack on his back.

'Are there any good children here?' he asked.

'Yes, there are good children here,' said Pip. 'But we have a real naughty boy too, whose name is Lars. He seems to be out at the moment, thank goodness.'

'I've heard about him,' said Santa Claus. 'He's the nicest boy in this country. He should have more presents than anyone else.'

But he didn't get any more than anyone else. We all got the same number of presents. I got a new doll, and three books, a game, a piece of cloth for a dress, mittens, and all kinds of other things. I got fifteen presents altogether.

I had made a tea cloth with cross stitch for Mother. She was very happy when she got it. I had bought a calendar for Father. He was happy too. I like it when people are happy about the Christmas presents I give them. It's as much fun as getting presents yourself. I gave tin soldiers to Lars and Pip.

Afterwards we danced round the tree, and everyone from North Farm and South Farm came and helped us. Grandpa came too, although he couldn't dance. I think we danced the polka and the barn dance at least twenty times.

That night I put all my Christmas presents on the table by my bed, so that I'd be able to see them first thing when I woke up in the morning.

Christmas is wonderful! It's a great pity that it isn't Christmas a little more often.

12. Waiting for the New Year

On the morning of New Year's Eve, when I was having breakfast in the kitchen, Britta and Anna came in. They looked excited, and Britta said, 'Lisa, do you want to wait up for the New Year with us?'

'Oh, yes, of course I do,' I said.

But first I had to ask Mother if I could stay up until midnight, when the New Year comes in. She said I could, so we decided right away that we would wait up for it in my room. Mother said that she would give us apples and nuts and ginger beer so we could have a real feast.

A few minutes later Lars and Pip came in, and I said, 'Britta and Anna and I are going to wait up and watch for the New Year tonight!'

Lars said, 'So are we. We decided that a long time ago.'

But I'm sure he decided to wait up for the New Year just because we were going to.

We ran over and asked Grandpa if he wanted to wait up with us, but he said that he always got too sleepy at night. Grandpa is so very, very nice! He went to his cupboard and got several little pieces of lead which he gave us.

'You can't have a real New Year's wake without melting lead,' he said.

He told us that you can find out what's going to happen to you during the coming year if you melt lead and pour it into cold water. If the lead takes the shape of a coin, for instance, it

means that you'll get a lot of money. Grandpa let us borrow a little ladle the boys use when they cast lead soldiers.

We didn't tell the boys that Grandpa had given us the lead.

We had fun that evening! My room was all ready for the party. I had taken out the rag carpets and beaten them, and had dusted everywhere. I had a pretty candlestick with five candles that I put in the centre of the table, with the bowl of apples and the jug of ginger beer and the dish of nuts arranged round it.

When Britta and Anna arrived, the candles were burning beautifully. I had a fire burning in the fireplace too.

'I like New Year's wakes!' said Anna.

The boys were waiting for the New Year in Lars' and Pip's room. A big dark attic separates their room from mine, and just as we had settled down to wait we heard footsteps there. A little while later we heard a terrible bang, but we didn't pay any attention to it. We knew that it was the boys who were trying to lure us out into the attic. We had heard Lars' cap pistol before.

After that nothing more happened, so we began to get curious and peeped out through a crack in our door. The attic was perfectly quiet and dark. Then we decided to creep across and look through the boys' keyhole to see what they were doing.

'I don't see a thing,' said Britta, who looked first. 'They aren't even there.'

'I shouldn't be surprised if they've gone to sleep and forgotten all about the New Year,' said Anna.

'Well they're certainly the ones to hold New Year's wakes,' I said. 'Let's get one of Lars' caps and wake them up.'

Suddenly something went bang right behind us, and we were so startled that we nearly jumped out of our skins.

'Those villains are hiding in the attic,' cried Anna.

I ran for my flashlight, and we flashed it in all the corners and behind all the old trunks and clothes, but found no boys.

'This is most peculiar,' said Britta.

There was another loud bang right behind us. It was a firework this time.

'Just wait until I get hold of that Lars,' said Britta fiercely. 'I'll give him a beating he'll never forget.'

'Yes, do that, by all means.' Lars' voice came from high over our heads.

And up there on the beams under the ceiling sat Lars and Pip and Olaf. We were furious.

'How's your old New Year's wake going?' Lars asked.

'Very well, thank you,' we said. 'We are just going to start melting lead to see what's going to happen next year.'

That made them curious, I can tell you. They followed us to my room, and when they saw how nice it looked with candles and a fire and everything, they decided to move over with us. Pip brought their apples and nuts and ginger beer.

Then we melted the lead in the ladle in the fireplace, and each one poured a little into the water in my washbasin. Lars poured first. When his chunk of lead had hardened, he fished it out and examined it carefully. Then he said, 'It looks as if I were going to become a king, because this is a king's crown.'

Anna laughed. 'It looks more like a book to me! That means that you're going to have to go to school all of next year.'

My chunk of lead was funny-looking. 'I think it's a bicycle,' said Olaf.

That made me happy, because I want a bicycle very, very much.

When we'd finished pouring lead we sat down on the floor in front of the fireplace and told stories. Britta tells *such* good stories. We ate lots of apples and nuts and drank ginger beer. And then we 'nutted'. Britta and Anna knew a wonderful way to do it. Britta held some nuts in her hand, but we didn't know how many.

First Britta said, 'The stove is smoking!'

And then Anna answered, 'I'll have to run up to the attic!'

And then Britta asked, 'How many boys will you take with you?'

'Five,' said Anna. Britta had exactly five nuts in her hand, she had to give them to Anna, and Anna had won the nutting. We nutted in lots of other ways too, but Anna was so clever that when we finished she had twice as many nuts as anyone else.

All at once Pip began to yawn. Finally he said that he was going to lie down on my bed to wait for the New Year. He did lie down, but it wasn't two minutes before he was fast asleep. Mother and Father came to say good night to us, because they weren't going to stay up till midnight.

A little later we asked Lars what time it was.

'Half past ten,' he said.

I think New Year's Eve is probably longer than other nights.

It seemed as if midnight would never come. But finally it did. We tried to wake up Pip to tell him the New Year had arrived, but that was absolutely impossible. We turned out the light and stood by the window, looking out into the darkness to see if the New Year was riding in. We couldn't see a thing. But anyway we drank ginger beer and cried, 'Happy New Year!'

We decided that we would have a New Year's wake every year because it was so much fun.

I was beginning to feel that I wanted nothing on earth so much as to go to bed – but there was Pip, fast asleep. We all carried him by his arms and legs to his own bed. He didn't wake up at all. Lars undressed him and put on his pyjamas and then tied one of my hair ribbons in his hair.

'We'll leave it there until tomorrow so Pip can see that he had a good time at the New Year's wake,' said Lars.

13. Aunt Jenny's party

The most fun during our whole holiday was the party the Sunday after Christmas at Aunt Jenny's. She lives on a farm on the other side of the big village.

Everybody in Bullerby was invited, and we had to ride for hours to get there. There was a sleigh from each farm.

Mother woke us up very early and bundled us up in an awful lot of sweaters and scarves. I was sure I should suffocate before I got to the party, but then Mother came with still another shawl to put over my head! I said that if I had to go to Aunt Jenny's looking like a freak, I wouldn't go at all.

We rode in our wicker sleigh with Father driving. Behind us came the South Farm sleigh, and the North Farm sleigh came last. All the bells sounded very gay. We were so happy that we began to sing, but Mother said we had to stop because we'd get too much cold air in our lungs. So instead we shouted a lot of messages to Olaf, who was in the sleigh behind us, and he yelled them on to Britta and Anna.

'If she gives us herring salad, I'm going home,' yelled Lars.

'So am I,' yelled Olaf.

Then Olaf explained to Britta and Anna what they were talking about, and after a while Olaf yelled to us that Britta and Anna would also go home if they had to eat herring salad.

We did have herring salad, but we didn't go home, because there were a great many other kinds of food and we didn't have to eat the herring salad.

Aunt Jenny has three girls of her own, and there were crowds of other children at the party. We played in a big room on the second floor all day long except when we ate. We really got tired of all that food, because as soon as we had started on a new game, Aunt Jenny would come and tell us that now we had to go down and eat some more. Grown-ups don't seem to do *anything* but eat when they're at a party.

Aunt Jenny's oldest girl's name is Nancy. We pretended that Nancy was a witch who lived in a cupboard next to the playroom. The cupboard was her cottage, and the playroom was a large forest. Just as we were walking through the forest, picking berries, out came the witch from her cottage and caught us. We were as scared as if she had been a real witch! There was a big box in the cupboard, and this was the witch's oven. She tried to cook Lars in it, but he got out just at the last minute, thank goodness.

'I do smell a little burned, though,' said Lars.

Sometimes the witch rushed at us and cried, 'Petrified!'

When she said this everyone had to stop perfectly still in the middle of whatever he was doing and not move a muscle. Once when the witch cried, 'Petrified,' Lars was caught standing on one leg with his tongue stuck out, his fingers poked in his ears, and his eyes crossed.

He had to stand still, looking like that, until the witch came and broke the spell. How we laughed at him!

Aunt Jenny's girls had a beautiful dolls' house in the corner of the playroom. Anna and I couldn't help going over there to look at it every few minutes. There was a kitchen in the dolls' house and a dining room and a bedroom and a living room. A very fine doll family lived there. Nancy said their names were Count and Countess Goldenmushroom. They had a pretty little girl who sat in a chair in the living room, whose name was Isabella Goldenmushroom.

When the grown-ups had finally finished eating, they came up and played with us too. First we played blind man's bluff. Then we played pawn games. I gave my little gold heart as a pawn. To get it back I was sentenced to turn three somersaults. I did, and then I got my gold heart.

Olaf was sentenced to say the name of his beloved three times into the fireplace, and just think, he said 'Lisa' three times. Lars started to laugh, and I was terribly embarrassed. But Olaf looked full of mischief and said to me, 'I meant my mother, of course. Her name is Lisa too.'

Father was sentenced to jump around the whole room like a frog. I had never seen Father jump like a frog before, and it was terribly funny! But the worst sentence was Aunt Jenny's. She was told to climb up on the table, stand on one leg, and crow like a rooster. She wouldn't do it, though.

'Nonsense,' she said. 'How could the table hold me, fat as I am?'

She was probably right. Aunt Jenny weighs almost two hundred pounds.

We played for a long time and had a lot of fun. But now and then Anna and I stole over to the dolls' house to say hello to Isabella Goldenmushroom.

The best thing about Aunt Jenny's party was that we were going to stay all night. I like to spend the night in strange houses; everything feels so different and wonderful. It also smells quite different from home.

There were fourteen of us children at the party, and we were all going to sleep in a row on the floor in the playroom. Just think what fun it was to lie on the floor! We had straw mattresses but no sheets, just blankets. When we had gone to bed, all the grown-ups came up to look at us.

'Here lies Sweden's youth by the yard,' said Father.

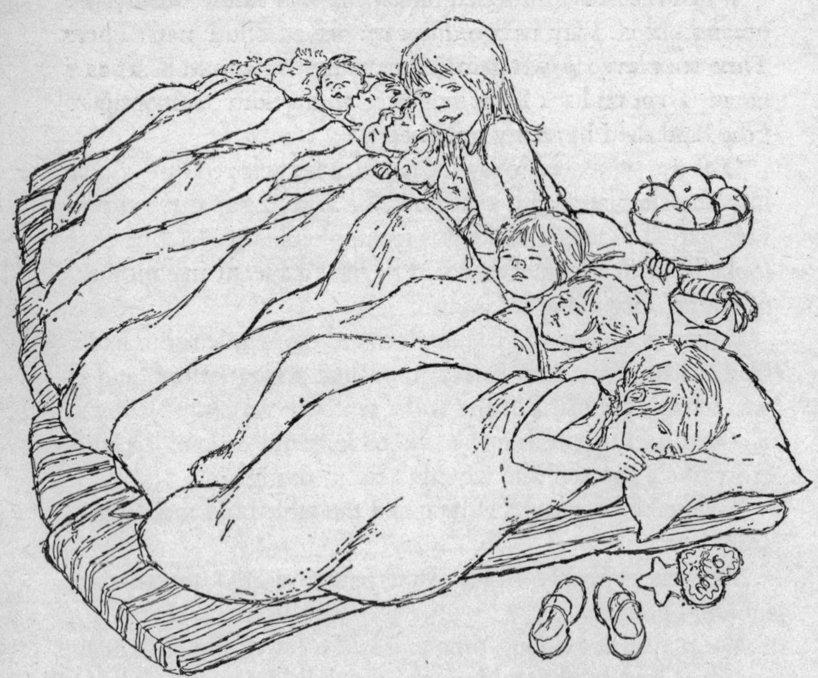

When the grown-ups had left, we were supposed to go to sleep. But I think it's almost impossible to get fourteen children to be quiet enough for anyone to be able to sleep.

Nancy told us about a big treasure that some knight had buried near there long, long ago. Lars wanted to go out and dig for it in the middle of the night. But Nancy said that nobody could find the treasure because it was bewitched. Then

I must have gone to sleep because I don't remember hearing any more.

We didn't go home until late in the afternoon of the next day. It was quite dark before we got to our village. We didn't yell from one sleigh to another on the way home because we were so tired. I lay back and looked up at all the stars. There were so many of them, and they were so far away. Then I crept down under the fur rug and sang quietly to myself, so that Lars and Pip would not hear me:

Twinkle, twinkle, little star,
How I wonder what you are.

I hope that we can go to a Christmas party at Aunt Jenny's next year too.

14. Lars falls into the lake

If you run right through the cow pasture at North Farm, you come to a little lake where we skate in the winter. Last year there was lovely glassy ice on the lake.

One day Mother didn't want us to go to the lake because Father and Uncle Erik had cut out a large hole to get ice for all of us. But I said, 'They put juniper branches round the hole, so we'll know where it is and keep away from it.'

So she let us go.

Sometimes Lars is rather silly, especially when he tries to show off as he did that day on the ice. He skated as close to the hole as he could.

'Here comes the Master Skater from Bullerby,' he cried. He skated straight towards the hole and did not turn off until the very last moment.

'Stop it, Lars, you're really acting like a goof,' said Olaf. We all shouted at him, but it didn't help.

'Here he comes, the brave Master Skater from Bullerby,' he said again.

Well, he certainly did come! In fact he splashed right down into the hole because he had come too close to the edge.

We all screamed. And Lars screamed too, worse than anyone else. We got frightened and thought he would drown. Then we lay down on the ice in a long line and held on to each other's feet. Pip was at the head of the line, right at the edge of the hole, and with all of us holding him, he pulled Lars up out of the hole. Lars *almost* cried but not quite.

We ran home as fast as we could.

'Just think if we had brought you home drownded,' Pip said.

'You don't say "drownded", stupid,' Lars answered. But I still think he liked Pip for pulling him out, because later in the afternoon he gave him a whole lot of tin soldiers.

Mother was quite angry at Lars for falling into the hole. He had to go to bed and drink hot milk. And afterwards Mother made him stay in bed several hours – to think about his sins, she said.

But that evening Lars got up to play with us in the snow. We built snow forts out in the yard and had a snowball battle. The girls had one fort, and the boys had another. But the boys made such hard snowballs and threw them so fast, that I didn't think it was fair. They came storming towards our fort with their hands full of snowballs, and Lars cried, 'Battle and victory! Here comes the Terror of the Northland!'

So Britta said, 'So that's who it is! I thought it was the Master Skater from Bullerby!'

After that Lars didn't say anything for quite a while.

The boys captured our fort and made us prisoners and said we had to sit and make snowballs for them all evening.

'What are you going to do with all those snowballs?' Anna said.

'Save them until Midsummer, because then they will be very rare,' Lars said.

And then Britta and Anna and I got cold, so we went down to the barn. It was nice and warm in there. We played catch, and before long the boys came down too. The cows stared at us all the time. I don't think that cows can understand why you play catch. Come to think about it, I don't understand it either, but it's fun.

After a while, Father came to the barn. He said we couldn't play catch any longer, because one of the cows was about to have a calf, and there mustn't be any noise and confusion.

Lotta was the one who was going to have the calf. We went to see it very soon after it was born. It was a little bull calf, and he was sweet. Lotta licked him and looked very happy.

Father wanted us to help him think of a name for the calf.

'Let's call him the Terror of the Northland,' Lars said.

What a stupid name for such a dear little calf! I don't think Lars can think of anything else except old Terror of the Northland.

'Well, he'll be a fierce, dangerous bull when he grows up, won't he?' Lars said.

Then Olaf suggested that we call the calf Peter, and Father thought that that would be a good name.

'Let's at least call him Peter from the Northland,' Lars said.

Then we ran over to tell Grandpa that Lotta had a calf.

Very soon after that it was bedtime. Lars and Pip and I were standing in the attic, and I was about to go into my room, when Lars teased Pip and said, 'I guess I'm lucky not to be "drownded", after all.'

'Oh, go and jump in the lake,' said Pip.

15. Those mischievous boys

When the Christmas holidays were over, there was still so much snow that we could ride our push-sleighs to school. We have three push-sleighs. Sometimes we fastened all three together to make one long sleigh with several seats.

Miss Johnson, our teacher, said it was nice to see us again, and I thought it was nice to see her too because I like her so much. She treated all the children to sweets because it was the first day of school. She'd bought the sweets in Stockholm, where she spent her holiday. That's the only time I've ever eaten sweets bought in Stockholm.

It was fun to see all the children from the big village again. During break the girls traded bookmarks as usual. I traded with Anna-Greta, a girl in our class who has many, many bookmarks. I gave her a basket of flowers and a Santa Claus bookmark, and she gave me a princess. It was almost the prettiest bookmark I had ever seen, so I think I made a good bargain.

In the winter the boys usually throw snowballs at each other during break. In the spring they play marbles, and the girls play hopscotch. When the boys have nothing else to do they fight, and during class they get into all kinds of mischief, whether it's winter or spring. Miss Johnson says she thinks there is something that makes boys' fingers itch so they can't help doing mischief. I think that Lars' fingers must itch all the time!

One day he brought to school a funny little pig that Pip had

given him. It was made of rubber, and you could blow it up. When you let the air out, the pig squealed loudly.

Our class was reading – reading is my favourite subject – and it was my turn to read aloud. The story was about Gustaf Vasa.

'Then the king dissolved in tears,' I said. And just as I spoke the words we heard a long, sad wail that sounded like Gustaf Vasa dissolving in tears. But it wasn't; it was Lars' pig.

All the children laughed, and Miss Johnson looked as if she were going to laugh too, but she didn't. Lars had to stand in the corner for the rest of the lesson period. So did the pig.

But Lars isn't the only one who gets into mischief. All the boys are about the same. One day Miss Johnson had to go to a teachers' meeting, and we were supposed to go on with drawing and arithmetic by ourselves. Miss Johnson told Britta to sit at her desk and take charge.

But Miss Johnson hadn't more than stepped outside the door when the boys started to act up.

'Miss Britta, Miss Britta,' they called and waved their hands.

'What do you want?' said Britta.

'We want to go out,' they all yelled.

And Pip said, 'Have you heard, Miss Britta, that the potatoes are growing well this year?'

Britta said, 'Yes, I think I have heard that.'

And Pip said, 'Then you must have very good ears, Miss Britta.'

Lars raised his hand and asked if he couldn't show Miss Britta what he had been drawing. He took his drawing pad to Britta, and the whole page was covered with black crayon.

'What is this supposed to be?' asked Britta.

'It's supposed to be five black cats in a dark cupboard,' said Lars.

Britta didn't think that it was any fun at all to be a teacher and she was glad when our real teacher came back. Miss Johnson asked if the children had been good. Britta said, 'Not the boys.'

So Miss Johnson scolded the boys and said they would all

have to stay after school a whole hour and do arithmetic. And do you know, during break a boy named Steve went over to Britta and said, 'Tattletale, tattletale!' and hit her over the head with his schoolbag. Wasn't that mean!

When we were walking home Britta told Anna and me that she never wanted to be a teacher again in her whole life.

We walked as slowly as we could so that Lars and Pip and Olaf could catch up with us. We knew that if they got home a whole hour later than we did our mothers would probably wonder what had happened, and the boys would be punished again.

16. Easter in Bullerby

Now I'm going to tell you about last Easter in Bullerby.

On Easter Eve, Mother and Father were going to a party at the minister's in the big village, so they let Lars and Pip and me have an egg party at our house.

Mother owns the Bullerby chicken farm, and so we have a great many eggs.

Pip thinks his hen Albertina lays almost all the eggs.

We ate supper in the kitchen. The table looked beautiful, with a blue cloth and our yellow Easter plates. There were birch branches in a vase, and Lars and Pip and I had painted all the eggs red and yellow and green.

Eggs should be those colours all the time, I think, because they look so nice.

We had written verses on the eggs.

> Anna, you must eat this in a flash,
> Or you might get corned-beef hash,

it said on one of the eggs.

Lars had written that verse, but Pip didn't think it was very good.

'Who ever thought of giving anyone corned-beef hash for Easter?' he said.

'How do you know what people might have thought of giving for Easter?' said Lars.

'This is an egg for Ann,
Instead of a frying pan.

Do you think that is better?' he asked.

Pip didn't think so. Anyway, we didn't have time to change the verse because just then Britta and Anna and Olaf arrived. At supper we had a race to see who could eat the most eggs. I could only eat three, but Olaf ate six.

'Albertina is a good hen,' Pip said when we had finished. Afterwards we were going to hunt for the Easter eggs filled with sweets which Mother had hidden.

Every Easter Eve, Lars and Pip and I each get a large egg filled with lots and lots of sweets. But this year Mother said that if we would be satisfied with eggs that were a little smaller, she would buy some for Britta and Anna and Olaf too. Then we could give them as a surprise at our party. Of course we wanted to do this.

It was very hard to find all the Easter eggs, Mother had hidden them so cleverly. Mine was in the cupboard where we keep the pots and pans. It was made of silver with little flowers. Inside there was a little chicken made of almond paste, and lots of sweets.

We were allowed to stay up as long as we wanted to, since it was Easter Eve. Agda, our maid, was out with Oscar, the farm hand, and we were alone in the house, so we turned out all the lights and played hide-and-seek in the dark. We counted 'Eeny, meeny, miney, mo,' and Pip was the first one to be blindfolded. I found a good hiding place in the dining-room

window behind the curtain. Pip tiptoed right by me several times, but he didn't find me.

But Britta was the one who found the best hiding place of all.

Father's rubber boots stood out in the hall, and on a hook above them hung the big coat that he wears when he drives to the dairy every day with the milk.

Well, Britta climbed down in the boots and wrapped the coat round her.

When we couldn't find Britta anywhere, we turned on the lights and all of us hunted for her, but we still couldn't find her. Then we called, 'You're free to come out!' But she just stood there, quiet as a mouse. Father's boots and coat looked just as usual, so how could we dream that Britta was inside them?

'Perhaps she is dead and gone for ever,' said Olaf.

Then we heard a giggle from inside the coat, and Britta stepped out, wearing Father's big boots. She wanted to play Puss in Boots, but Anna said it was time to go over to Grandpa's and make eggnog. So we did.

We took eggs and sugar and glasses to Grandpa's room.

Grandpa was sitting in his big rocking chair in front of the fire, and he was very glad when we came.

We all sat down on the floor in front of the fire and whipped eggnog very hard so that it splashed round us.

Anna whipped Grandpa's for him because he couldn't see to do it himself.

I told him about my Easter egg made of silver with little flowers.

Then Grandpa told us about the olden days when children didn't have any Easter eggs filled with sweets.

And do you know that one Easter, when Grandpa was a

little boy, it was so cold that his daddy had to use an axe to break the ice on the barrel of water that stood in the kitchen? And there were no Easter eggs to cheer him up!

Poor little Grandpa!

17. April Fools' Day

On the first of April we had fun fooling Miss Johnson, our teacher, as you should on April Fools' Day.

Well, perhaps you *shouldn't* do it, exactly, but you *can* do it, and you don't ever get punished for doing it.

Usually we start school at eight o'clock in the morning, but the day before April the first we all decided to go to school at six the next morning. Just before Miss Johnson locked the door of the schoolroom after our last lesson, Lars ran in and moved the hands of the clock in the schoolroom two hours ahead.

The next day we all got to school at six o'clock, but the clock on the wall in the schoolroom said eight.

We made all the noise we could outside the schoolroom door so that Miss Johnson would hear us. When she didn't come, Lars ran up to the second floor and knocked on her door. She lives over the school.

'Who is it?' asked Miss Johnson, in a sleepy voice.

'It's Lars,' he said. 'Aren't we going to have any school today?'

'My goodness, I've overslept,' said Miss Johnson. 'I'll be down in a minute.'

Miss Johnson has a clock up in her room too, of course, but she was in such a hurry that she forgot to look at it.

The clock in the schoolroom said twenty minutes past eight when Miss Johnson came down to let us in.

'I can't understand why my alarm clock didn't ring and wake me up,' she said.

My, how hard it was for us to keep from laughing when she said that!

We had arithmetic for the first lesson. And just as we were reciting the multiplication table, we heard the alarm clock ringing up in Miss Johnson's room upstairs.

It was really seven o'clock then. But the clock in the schoolroom showed nine.

'What now?' said Miss Johnson.

'April fool! April fool!' we all yelled.

It's only on the first of April that you can say things like that to your teacher.

'Such children!' Miss Johnson said.

When we had had all the lessons that we were supposed to have that day, we thought, of course, that we would be allowed to go home, although it was only one o'clock. But then Miss Johnson said, 'April fool! Now we'll have school for another hour.'

So we had to stay at school for another hour. But it didn't matter, because Miss Johnson read stories to us.

On the way home Olaf suddenly said to Lars, 'Why Lars, how did you get that big hole in the seat of your pants?'

Lars turned his head almost clear round trying to see the hole. When he had been looking for a while Olaf said, 'April fool! April fool!'

Olaf was so pleased that he had been able to fool Lars. And he was still in the mood for fooling people when we met that mean shoemaker who lives halfway between the big village and Bullerby – the one whose name is Good, but who isn't good but very cantankerous.

'Look, Mr Good,' said Olaf. 'Look at the fox over there in the bushes!'

But Mr Good didn't even look over that way; he only said, 'And look at the bunch of trouble-making brats walking down the road.'

Then Lars laughed.

In the afternoon, when we had done our homework, Lars ran over to South Farm and said to Olaf, 'There's a scrap dealer over at North Farm and he's buying stones.'

'He buys stones?' said Olaf, who had completely forgotten that it was April Fools' Day. 'What kind of stones?'

'The kind of stones you have here in your garden, I suppose,' said Lars.

Olaf started picking up stones for dear life and putting them in a sack. Then he lugged the sack over to North Farm. There really was an old man over there, but he only bought empty bottles and other kinds of scrap.

'Here are some more stones for you,' said Olaf. He pulled the sack up to the old man, looking pleased with himself.

'Stones?' said the old man. 'Did you say stones?'

'Sure,' said Olaf, and looked still more pleased. 'First-class granite too. I've picked them myself in our garden.'

'Is that so?' said the old man. 'Well, I'm afraid someone's been pulling your leg, my lad.'

Then Olaf remembered that it was April Fools' Day. He

got very red in the face and took his sack and dragged it home without saying a word. But Lars stood behind the fence and yelled, 'April Fool! April Fool!' so loudly that you could hear him all over Bullerby.

18. Anna and I go shopping

The shop where we buy sugar and coffee and things like that is in the big village, close to the school. When Mother needs some groceries she usually asks me to get them for her after school. But during the summer holidays we have to make a special trip. One day Mother said, 'Lisa, there's no help for it. You'll have to run down to the shop for me.'

It was a beautiful day, and I thought it would be fun to go shopping, so I said, 'Of course, I'd love to. What do you want?'

Mother said we'd probably better write a list. But we couldn't find a pencil, so I said, 'Never mind. I can remember it all.'

Then Mother told me all the things I should buy: six ounces of yeast and a piece of Bologna sausage of the best quality, a package of ginger, some sewing needles, a tin of anchovies, a bag of almonds and a bottle of vinegar.

'I'm sure I'll remember it all,' I said.

Just then Anna came rushing into our kitchen and asked me if I'd go to the shop with her.

'Yes,' I said. 'I was just going to ask you to come with me.'

Anna was wearing her new red cap and carried a basket on her arm. I put on my new green cap and took a basket on my arm too.

Anna was going to buy soap, a pound of coffee, two pounds of sugar, and two yards of elastic tape. Also she was to get a piece of Bologna sausage of the best quality, just as I was. Anna hadn't written down what she was going to buy either.

Before we left we went up to Grandpa's room to ask if there was anything he needed from the shop, and he asked us to buy him some barley-sugar and a bottle of camphor liniment.

Just as we were leaving through the gate, Olaf's mother came running out on to their porch.

'Are you going to the shop?' she called.

'Yes,' we said.

'Oh, please would you buy a few things for me?' she asked.

We said we'd love to. She wanted us to buy a spool of white thread, number 40, and a bottle of vanilla essence.

'And wait, what else was it I wanted?' she said, looking thoughtful.

'A piece of Bologna sausage of the best quality?' I suggested.

'Yes, that was it,' said Olaf's mother. 'How could you guess?'

Then Anna and I left, and we were a little worried for fear we wouldn't be able to remember everything. First we recited all the things to each other out loud, but we soon got tired of that. We walked along arm in arm, swinging our baskets back and forth. The sun was shining and the trees smelled good. Then we made up songs about what we were to get. We sang, as loudly as we could, 'A piece of Bologna sausage of the best quality.' It sounded quite pretty. This is the way we did it. First I sang, 'A piece of Bologna sausage,' in a slow, romantic melody, and then Anna struck up, 'Of the best quality, of the best quality,' in a fast, happy tune. Sometimes we sang the words in a melody that was good to march to. But finally we settled for one that was sad all the way through and very beautiful. It was so beautiful that we almost began to cry.

'My, how sad it is about Bologna sausage,' Anna said when we finally reached the shop.

There were a lot of people in the shop so we had to wait a long time, really much longer than we should have, because grown-ups seem to think that it doesn't matter how long children have to wait. They always push ahead. But finally Uncle Emil himself came out into the shop. We know him. He started to ask how everyone in Bullerby was, and if we had eaten lots of eggs at Easter, and if we weren't going to get married soon.

'We certainly are *not*,' we said.

'And what do the ladies wish to buy today?' asked Uncle Emil. He always talks silly like that, but I like him all the same. He has a pencil behind his ear and a little red moustache. He always treats us to aniseed balls that he keeps in a big jar.

First Anna told him everything that she was supposed to buy for her mother and for Grandfather. Uncle Emil weighed everything and wrapped it in packages while Anna talked.

Then it was my turn to tell him everything I was going to get for Mother and Olaf's mother. Both Anna and I thought as hard as we could so that we wouldn't forget anything. Uncle Emil gave us two aniseed balls apiece, and we left.

When we had walked as far as the fork in the road where we turn to Bullerby, I said, 'Anna, do you remember if I bought yeast?'

Anna couldn't at all remember. We started squeezing all the packages in my basket. There was nothing that felt like yeast. So we had to go back to the store. Uncle Emil laughed at us and gave us the yeast and some more aniseed balls. Then we left.

Just as we came to the fork in the road again, Anna cried, 'Grandpa's camphor liniment!'

'I've never seen the like!' I said.

There was nothing else we could do but go back to the store. How Uncle Emil laughed at us! He gave us the camphor liniment and still more aniseed balls.

When we came to the fork in the road the next time Anna looked so frightened that I felt sorry for her.

'Lisa,' she said. 'I'm almost sure that I didn't buy any sugar.'

'Anna,' I said, 'don't tell me that you didn't buy the *sugar*. You simply *must* have bought the sugar!'

We squeezed and squeezed the things in Anna's basket, but there was nothing which felt the least bit sugary.

Uncle Emil almost fell across the counter when he saw us again. But he gave us the sugar and still more aniseed balls.

'I'd better get out a spare jar of aniseed balls,' he said, 'because my whole stock is disappearing.'

'Don't worry, we shan't come back any more,' said Anna.

Just before we came to the fork in the road again I said, 'Anna, let's *run* past the fork. It's the only way to get by. Otherwise we'll think of something else that we've forgotten.'

So we ran by the fork.

'It worked!' said Anna. At last we were on our way home.

'Let's sing a little more,' said Anna.

We did. We started with 'A piece of Bologna sausage of the best quality,' and it sounded just as beautiful and sad as before. Anna said that we ought to introduce that song at school and sing it at speech day next year. We sang and sang and sang while we struggled up the hill towards Bullerby.

And then – just as I bellowed, 'A piece of Bologna sausage,' extra beautifully – Anna took me by the arm and looked absolutely wild.

'Lisa,' she said, 'we haven't bought any Bologna sausage!'

We sat down by the side of the road and didn't say anything for a long while. Then Anna said that she wished no one had ever invented Bologna sausages.

'Why can't people eat frankfurters instead?' she said.

My, how long the road back seemed this time. We didn't

sing any more. Anna said she did not think that song about the Bologna sausage was at all suitable to sing at school.

'No,' I said, 'not at school and not any other place either. What a ridiculous song!'

When Uncle Emil saw us he held his head, and then he ran to get a new jar of aniseed balls. But we said that no, thank you, we didn't care for any more aniseed balls.

'Really?' said Uncle Emil. 'What do you want, then?'

'Three pieces of Bologna sausage of the best quality,' we said.

'If there *is* such a thing as good Bologna sausage,' Anna muttered.

We dragged ourselves homewards. But when we came to the fork in the road Anna looked back and said, 'Look, there comes John from the mill, driving his ugly old tawny mare!' John works in a mill that lies on the other side of Bullerby.

'May we have a ride?' we cried when John had caught up with us.

'Jump right in,' said John.

We jumped up on the flour sacks behind John and rode all the way to Bullerby. I started humming, 'A piece of Bologna sausage of the best quality,' but Anna said, 'If you sing one more word of that song I'll push you off the wagon.'

When I came into the kitchen, Mother said, 'Goodness, Lisa, what a long time you've been gone!'

'No wonder,' I said. 'With all that Bologna sausage to buy.'

When Mother had taken all the things out of the basket she said, 'That was a good girl who remembered everything!'

19. Olaf has a sister

Sometimes when I get tired of Lars and Pip I think that it would be better not to have any brothers at all. They tease me when I play with my dolls; they're always hitting me; and they always say that it's my turn to dry the dishes. Lars once told Mother that he couldn't understand why anyone should have wanted to have a girl. It would have been much better to have had nine more boys, so they could have enough for a soccer team.

But Mother said, 'I am so happy to have my little girl. I don't know what I'd do without her. But nine more boys! It's quite enough with you two.'

So Lars didn't get anywhere with his stupid suggestion.

But sometimes it's nice to have brothers – when we have pillow fights at night, when they come into my room and tell ghost stories, and when it's Christmas and things like that. And once Pip stood up for me when a boy in school hit me because I pushed him by mistake. Pip hit him back and said, 'Don't you ever do that again!'

'Well, she doesn't have to push me,' said Ben. That was the other boy's name.

'That wasn't her fault. She didn't see you. She doesn't have eyes in the back of her head, stupid,' said Pip.

My, how I liked Pip then! So it really isn't too bad to have brothers, but, of course, it would be better to have sisters.

'The main thing is not to be an only child,' Olaf used to say.

Before Kerstin was born, he would get furious because he hadn't got any brothers or sisters.

'Other people can have children, but in this house we never have any,' he said angrily.

But then, over a year ago, a little sister came after all. Olaf was so happy. The day she was born he rushed in and said we had to come and look at her right away. So we did.

'There she is. Isn't she pretty?' Olaf said and looked terribly proud.

But she certainly *wasn't* pretty! She was all red and wrinkled and really looked awful, I thought. Never have I seen anyone so amazed as Lars was when he saw how Olaf's baby sister looked. He stood there with his eyes popping and his mouth wide open. But he didn't say anything.

'Yes, she's very pretty,' said Britta, and then we left.

Then Pip said, 'Poor Olaf! Imagine having a sister like that! You can't say that Lisa is any beauty, but at least she looks like a human being. Imagine how embarrassed Olaf will be when this poor thing starts school.'

About a month passed before we went back to South Farm. Every day Olaf told us how pretty his little sister was, and Lars always looked so funny when he said it. But then we were all invited to South Farm for the christening of Olaf's sister.

'Oh, that poor child,' said Lars on the way over. 'It would probably be best for her if she could just die while she is a baby.'

The dining room at South Farm looked lovely. There were flowers everywhere, because Olaf's sister had been born in the spring when there were primroses and lilies of the valley. There was a jug of birch leaves in the open fire-place, and the table was set. And Olaf was all dressed up. So were we. The minister stood in the dining room and waited.

All of a sudden the door opened, and Aunt Lisa came in carrying Olaf's little sister. Oh, how that baby had changed! She had large, dark blue eyes, and her face was all pink, and her mouth – well, I just can't tell you what a pretty little mouth she had! She wore a beautiful long white christening dress.

Lars looked just as amazed as when he had seen her the first time. 'Have you got a new one?' he whispered to Olaf.

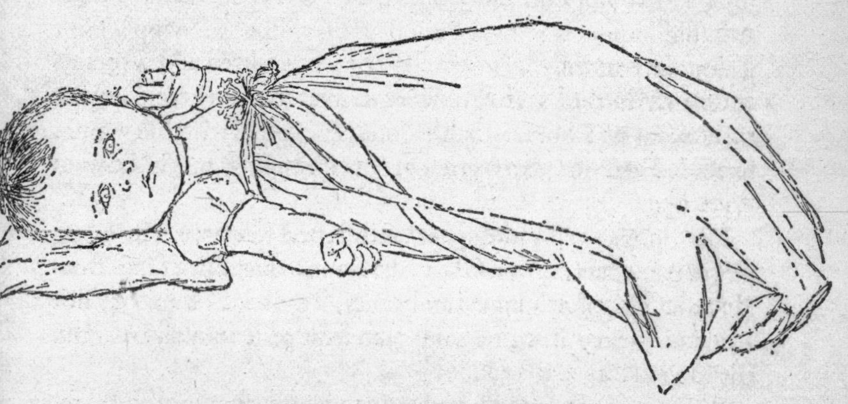

'A new one? What do you mean?' said Olaf.

'A new baby,' Lars said.

'What are you talking about?' said Olaf.

Then Lars didn't say anything more.

The minister christened Olaf's sister and named her Kerstin.

I love Kerstin! She is the prettiest baby in the world. Anna and Britta and I used to run over to South Farm almost every day to watch while Aunt Lisa took care of her. How she wiggled and kicked! – not Aunt Lisa, of course, but Kerstin. She looked so sweet. She wiggled most of all when she had her bath. She loved to take a bath.

Sometimes, when she lay in her cot, she almost talked, and

it sounded like 'ba, ba'. Olaf thought she would soon be able to say anything she wanted to.

When Olaf went to the cot to look at Kerstin, she would smile just as if she were happy to see him. She hadn't any teeth, but she still looked sweet when she smiled. Olaf's eyes sparkled when he looked at her.

Svipp, Olaf's dog, was a little jealous of Kerstin. He wants Olaf to like only him, of course. But Olaf petted Svipp a lot and told him he was a very good and fine dog, so Svipp wasn't jealous any more.

Once Aunt Lisa let Anna and me take care of Kerstin. Olaf wasn't at home, thank goodness; otherwise, he would have wanted to take care of her himself. This is how it happened.

Kerstin was lying in the cot, and started to cry like anything just as Aunt Lisa was about to take some loaves out of the oven. She was wet and hungry and cross – Kerstin, of course, not Aunt Lisa. So Aunt Lisa said, 'Do you girls think you could bath her?'

'Of course we could,' we said.

Anna brought out the bathtub and poured water into it. Aunt Lisa came and tested the water with her elbow, and I lifted Kerstin out of her cot. And, do you know, she stopped crying at once and started laughing instead. When I held her close to me, she nibbled my cheek. It didn't hurt, because she didn't have any teeth, you know. My face got all wet, but that didn't matter.

Aunt Lisa has taught me how to hold babies. You should hold them so that their backs get support; I also know how you should hold them when you give them a bath, so they won't get their heads under the water. So I held Kerstin while Anna washed her with the washcloth. Kerstin wiggled and

kicked and said 'ba, ba'. Then she tried to suck the washcloth, but we didn't let her!

'She's so sweet that I could eat her up,' said Anna.

Anna had put a blanket on the kitchen table, and a bath towel to dry Kerstin with. When I had finished bathing Kerstin, I put her on the blanket very carefully. We wrapped her in the towel, and Anna and I helped each other dry her. Then we sprinkled her all over with talcum powder.

Suddenly Kerstin put her big toe in her mouth and started sucking it, but we had to take her toe away from her when we started to put on her little vest. Aunt Lisa helped us to put on her nappy, because that was a little harder, but we put her pants on her by ourselves. When she was all ready, Aunt Lisa fed her.

Afterwards Aunt Lisa let Anna and me take Kerstin for a ride in her perambulator. We pretended that Anna was the daddy and I the mummy and Kerstin our little baby. It wasn't long before Kerstin went to sleep. But we still pushed her around and had such fun.

When Olaf came home, he rushed up and took away the pram, just as if he had thought we were stealing Kerstin. But when he had pushed her pram for a while, he let us hold the handle too and help push. We told Olaf that Kerstin had sucked her big toe, and Olaf laughed and said, 'No one would believe how many tricks that child can do. Perhaps she'll be in the circus when she grows up.'

Just then Kerstin woke up and looked at Olaf. He tickled her under the chin and said, 'Well, well, you little rascal. So you were sucking your big toe, were you?'

Then he laughed again and looked still more proud – just as if the finest thing you could do in this world was to suck your big toe.

20. I get a baby lamb

Anna and I sometimes try to work out at which time of year we have the most fun. Anna thinks we have the most fun in the summer, and I think in the spring – except for Christmas, of course.

Now I'm going to tell you about one thing that happened last spring. We have a lot of sheep here in Bullerby, and in the spring the ewes have baby lambs. The lambs are very sweet – sweeter than kittens or puppies or piglets.

During the time when the sheep have their babies, we run down to the sheep barn every morning to see how many new lambs have been born during the night.

As soon as you open the door, all the sheep begin to baa at the top of their voices. The baby lambs baa very sweetly and not at all like the ewes and the ram, whose voices are loud and deep.

One Sunday morning when I went down to the sheep barn, I found a baby lamb dead in the straw. I ran and told Father right away, and he found out why the lamb had died. His mother didn't have any milk to give him.

I sat down on the threshold of the sheep barn and cried to think about the poor baby lamb. Anna came over, and when I told her about it, she cried too.

'I don't want baby lambs to die,' I said to Father.

'Nobody does,' Father said. 'And I'm afraid there's still another one that won't live very long.' And he showed us a little lamb that he was carrying in his arms. It was the dead lamb's brother and, of course, he couldn't get any milk from his mother either.

When we heard this, Anna and I started crying even more.

'I don't want the little lamb to die,' I cried and threw myself on the ground.

Father lifted me up and said, 'Don't cry, Lisa.' Then he said,

'I'll tell you what, you may try to feed this lamb with a bottle, just as you would a baby.'

I don't think I'd ever been so happy before! I didn't know that you could feed lambs the way you do babies. Father said I mustn't be too sure. He thought that the lamb would probably die anyway, but we could always try.

Anna and I ran down to Aunt Lisa's and borrowed a teat and a bottle that Olaf had drunk milk from when he was a baby. Then we ran back to Father.

'Father, can't we give him a little cream, the poor little thing,' I said.

But Father said that his tummy could only take milk that was mixed with water. We mixed the milk, and then we heated the bottle in warm water. Then I stuck the teat in the lamb's mouth, and he started to suck right away he was so hungry.

'Now you are the foster mother of this little lamb,' said Father. 'But he has to have food early and late, so you mustn't get tired of feeding him.'

Anna said that if I did get tired she would do it for me. But I said, 'Don't worry. No one could get tired of feeding a baby lamb.'

I named the lamb Pontus, and Father said that he was my very own. It was lucky that all this was decided before Lars and Pip woke up that Sunday morning.

'To think that you can't even sleep late one morning without Lisa's getting a baby lamb!' said Lars, who was a little cross because he hadn't got Pontus.

The first few days every child in the village went with me to feed Pontus, but, before long, they got tired of it.

It's strange how hungry baby lambs are. Every morning, before I went to school, I would run down to the sheep barn to give Pontus his bottle. As soon as he saw me coming, he would run towards me, wagging his short little tail and baaing sweetly. He was all white, but he had a little black spot on his nose, so you could easily tell him from the other lambs.

Agda fed him during the day when I was at school. I gave him another bottle as soon as I got home. And late at night he had to be fed again.

I had promised Father that I wouldn't get tired of feeding Pontus, and I didn't, because I loved him so much. I loved him mainly because he was so happy when he saw me. I think he thought that I was his real mother. I asked Lars and Pip if they thought this was so, and Lars said, 'Yes, I'm sure he thinks so. You do look very much like a sheep.'

One day Father said it was time to try to teach Pontus to drink his milk from a bowl. He was getting too big to drink from a bottle.

Poor Pontus didn't know what he was supposed to do when I suddenly came and put a bowl under his nose. He nuzzled me to see where I had put the bottle.

Pip was watching.

'Drink the milk, for goodness' sake,' he said to Pontus. 'Are you stupid or something?'

I got furious with Pip. 'Pontus is certainly not stupid,' I said. 'You just don't understand baby lambs.'

But Pontus just sniffed at the milk and baaed and looked sad. Then I found the trick!

I dipped my hand in the milk, and when I put my fingers in Pontus' mouth he started to suck them. He sucked and he sucked, and, in that way, he drank all the milk – except for what he spilled. So for a while Pontus drank by sucking my fingers.

But one morning, when he was very hungry and couldn't get the milk from my fingers fast enough, he started drinking from the bowl. After that he always drank from the bowl. In a way this was too bad, because he was very sweet when he stood there and sucked the milk from my fingers.

A little later in the spring, the sheep were let out in the pasture to graze. The lambs were supposed to learn to eat grass, but they still had to have milk too, so I went to the sheep pasture every day with the bowl of milk. I would stand at the gate and yell 'Pontus!' as loudly as I could. Then I would hear a little baa from over the other side of the pasture, and Pontus would come running towards me at full speed wagging his stump of a tail back and forth.

But Pontus has grown so big now that he doesn't drink milk any more; he just eats grass and munches leaves. He is such a good lamb and eats so well that he is certain to grow up to be a big, strong ram some day.

Perhaps one day I'll get another lamb or perhaps a dog or a bird or a rabbit. But none of them will be as nice as Pontus. I'll never, never, never like any pet as much as I like Pontus!

21. Pontus goes to school

Lars used to tease me and always say, 'But it would be better to have a dog than a lamb.'

Olaf agreed with him, of course, because he has a dog himself.

'Naturally it's better to have a dog,' Olaf said.

'Why, may I ask?' I said.

'Well, for one thing, you can take a dog with you wherever you go,' Olaf said.

'All Pontus does is run round in the sheep pasture,' Lars said.

'But a lamb is much nicer,' said Anna to help me out.

'A lot of good that does you,' Lars said, 'when he only runs round the pasture.'

One morning after we had been talking about this the day before, I went, as usual, to the sheep pasture and called Pontus. When he came running he looked so sweet that I thought I wouldn't trade him for a thousand dogs. I also thought it a shame that he ran round in the pasture all the time with no one to see how sweet he was. Then I thought about Svipp.

Sometimes he follows Olaf to school. That's why Olaf said that dogs go with you everywhere. And once Miss Johnson let Svipp come into the school-room and lie on the floor by Olaf's desk.

But with poor Pontus it was quite different; he had to stay in the sheep pasture all day. While he drank his milk, I thought about how unfair it was that dogs were allowed to go everywhere but not lambs.

By the time Pontus had finished his milk, I had decided to let him come with me to school.

It's always hard for me to get ready in time for school when I have to go out and feed Pontus first. And on the morning when I was going to take him to school with me, I was so far behind that all the other children stood waiting for me outside Olaf's gate.

'Hurry up, Lisa,' Britta called, 'or we'll be late!'

Then I turned round and said to the lamb, 'Hurry up, Pontus, or we'll be late!'

Never have I seen any children look as surprised as they did when they saw Pontus!

'Where – where is he going?' said Lars.

'To school,' I said. 'And then perhaps we won't have to hear any more that only dogs can go anywhere.'

'Lisa, are you quite sure that you're not feeling ill?' said Lars.

'Do Mother and Father know about it?' Pip said.

When Pip asked that, I got a little worried, because it was something I hadn't thought about. But Anna clapped her hands and laughed and said, 'Why shouldn't lambs be allowed to go along to school as well as dogs?'

And all of a sudden Lars started to smile, and he said, 'Let him come along; Miss Johnson will probably faint.'

So then we trotted down the hills, all of us – Pontus too. Sometimes he stopped as if he wondered if this really was all right. But then I called 'Pontus!' and he said 'Baaa!' very sensibly and came along behind us.

It took us a little bit longer than usual to get to school, and we were late. The bell had already rung, and the other children had gone in.

Pontus stumbled going up the school steps, so I had to help a little.

'Perhaps he isn't mature enough for school yet,' Lars said.

When Lars first started at school several years ago, he couldn't sit still a minute. So Miss Johnson said that he wasn't mature enough for school yet and sent him home. She said that he could come back the next year, but first he had to play at home a little longer. Lars has never forgotten this. That's why he said that about Pontus.

Britta knocked on the school door, and we went in.

'I'm sorry we're late,' said Britta.

As soon as she had said it, Olaf started to giggle. All the rest

of us stood quietly, but he giggled as if someone were tickling him.

'You seem very happy today, Olaf,' said Miss Johnson.

Pontus stood at the back where no one could see him, but all of a sudden he said a little 'Baa!' and stuck his head between my leg and Lars'. All the children jumped out of their seats. Miss Johnson did too, for that matter.

'What in the world –' she said. 'You don't mean that you've brought a lamb to school?'

'Lisa –' Pip started, but then he was quiet, because he was

afraid Miss Johnson would get angry with me. I was beginning to get a little scared myself.

'Because we're studying domestic animals,' I said, 'I thought perhaps –'

'What did you think?' asked Miss Johnson.

'That it would be a good thing for the class to see a real lamb,' I said. But I really hadn't thought about it until just that minute.

Miss Johnson started to laugh like anything, and all the children too, especially Olaf. He laughed until he almost choked.

Then we took Pontus up to Miss Johnson's desk, and all the children were allowed to come and pet him. We read about sheep in our nature study book, and I told how I had raised Pontus with a bottle. Everyone liked him so much, and we sang 'Baa, baa, black sheep' to him.

I think Pontus himself was getting tired of all the noise and wanted to go back to the sheep pasture. But he was good and stayed very still beside my desk during the rest of the lesson. Well, sometimes he took a few small leaps and baaed. Every time he did, Olaf started to laugh, so that all the other children had to laugh too.

When the weather is warm and sunny we always eat our sandwiches on the school steps during lunch hour. We did that day. As usual I had brought milk in a bottle, so I gave it to Pontus in a bowl I had borrowed from Miss Johnson. Anna gave me half of her milk so that I wouldn't be without any.

Afterwards Pontus ran round the school yard. Once he started nibbling a few of the carrots that were starting to sprout in Miss Johnson's vegetable garden, but I chased him away from there and told him that he'd have to calm down until he got home.

When school was over and we were going home, Lars said, 'Tomorrow we are going to study cattle. That'll be fun, and I'll bring the bull.'

Then Olaf laughed until he got the hiccups.

'But it might be a little crowded to have him next to my desk,' Lars said.

Miss Johnson had said that now we had brought enough live animals to school. It could be a help when you were studying them, but it would be pretty confusing in the long run, she had said.

Pontus got tired on the way home, so we took turns carrying

him up all the hills. Then we all went to take him to the sheep pasture.

Never have I seen a lamb jump as high as Pontus did when we let him go! He galloped over to the other sheep and baaed so that you could hear him all over the pasture.

'It's quite clear that he isn't mature enough for school yet,' Lars said.

22. Walking home from school

We always have lots of fun when we walk home from school. It's a long walk, because the school is a long way away. We talk about everything that has happened at school, and we tell each other stories. We also talk about what we're going to do when we grow up, and things like that. Sometimes we sit down by the side of the road to rest, sometimes we climb trees, and sometimes we walk on top of the fence so the walk won't be so dull.

Mother says she can't understand why it takes more than twice as long to walk home as it does to walk to school. I don't understand it either. But it just can't be helped.

One day last spring, when we came home extra late, Mother said to me, 'Now tell me just exactly what you did on your way home.'

So I did. And this is what had happened.

First we went to the store and bought barley-sugar for Grandpa. We wanted to taste a little, but we knew that we shouldn't. Britta put it in her schoolbag and said, 'If all six of us tasted the barley-sugar, there wouldn't be any left in the bag for Grandpa.'

'That would never do,' said Lars. 'We'd better hurry home with it before something happens.'

We started off, but Pip was still thinking about the barley-sugar.

'I wish I had a lot of money!' he said. 'I'd spend it all on sweets.'

'Yes, but as it happens you haven't got any money,' said Anna.

'No, but what if I happened to find some?' said Pip.

'*You* couldn't happen to find anything,' said Britta, 'because you're always walking with your nose in the air. If you looked at the ground from time to time, perhaps you would find something.'

So Pip started to look at the ground. And sure enough he had not walked more than fifty yards before he found a krona, which is about seven pence in English money. We thought there were fairies who can hear what you wish and who walk around leaving money on the road. This krona was lying right in the road, where it forks off to Bullerby.

At first Pip just stood still, staring at the krona as if he thought it was a joke. But then he picked it up and ran back to the shop to buy some toffee, just as he had said he would. We waited at the fork, and when he came back we all got a toffee.

'Just think how easy it is to find money,' said Pip. 'My goodness, what piles of money I've been missing.'

After that we all walked along staring at the ground. Lars said. 'I wish I had a krona!'

He must have thought the fairy would give him a krona too. But he didn't find anything at all, so he said, 'I wish I had ten ore!' That's two pence in English money.

But he didn't even find that much. Then he said angrily, 'I bet I'll find at least one ore!'

But he didn't. Neither did anyone else. None of us has ever found even an ore since Pip found the krona.

Pip kept giving us toffees while we walked towards home. Then he got the idea of having a contest to see who could keep his toffee in his mouth the longest without its melting. He probably thought of that so the toffee would last longer.

Anyway, we all tried it. We each took a toffee and sucked it as slowly as we could. After a while we stood in a circle in the road and stuck out our tongues to compare our toffees. There was almost nothing left of them.

We were halfway to Bullerby by then and were standing right in front of Mr Good's cottage. He stuck his head out of the kitchen window and said we could take Agda's shoes to her. We pulled in our tongues quickly, because we didn't want him to see us comparing. Britta won the contest, and Lars put Agda's shoes in his satchel.

Then Olaf suggested that we should have a contest to see who could hold his breath the longest. But we waited until we were out of sight of the shoemaker's cottage, because he would have thought that was silly, too – to stand in the middle of the road and hold your breath.

We held our breath a long, long time. I told Mother afterwards that it wasn't because we held our breath so long that we had come home so late, but I was sure it had helped a little. Lars said that he won, but then Olaf said, 'No, you didn't! Pip was bluer in the face than you.'

The shoemaker has a meadow that floods in the spring and makes a little lake. There's a huge rock in the meadow and in the spring it sticks up out of the water like an island. When we got as far as the meadow, we stopped and rested a little while.

'I'd like to go out to that rock,' said Lars. We all said we would too. So Lars went and got a couple of fence poles that he put down as a bridge over to the rock. We crept over, one at a time. It was nice to sit out there on the rock in the sunshine.

'If we only had something to eat,' said Anna.

The toffee was all gone. Then Lars looked in his satchel.

There were Agda's shoes and a cheese sandwich that he hadn't been able to eat at lunchtime.

We pretended that the rock was a ship drifting round in the ocean, and that we were sailors who were going to die of starvation any day unless we were saved. Lars divided his sandwich into six equal parts for us. Then he said, 'Friends, this is the only thing that separates us from death. But you must be as brave as your captain.'

He was the captain, of course. Then he said the worst thing was that we had no water, so we should die of thirst too. But Pip said, 'As far as I can see there's plenty of water. This whole meadow is full of water!'

Lars said Pip was stupid. The water round our ship was salty, and he would shoot anyone who tried to drink it. If you drink salt water you go crazy, he said.

Then he lay down on the rock and pretended he was delirious from hunger and thirst, and Pip said, 'He must have drunk some salt water himself.'

Lars got down on his knees and folded his hands and shouted, 'Help, help!' as loudly as he could. In next to no time we heard someone running down the road, and it was the shoemaker! He thought Lars was really crying for help, and he was very cross.

'If you could get out there by yourselves, you can just get back by yourselves too,' he said. 'Dratted kids!'

But he walked out in the water all the same and lifted us down from the rock one at a time and put us up on dry land. Of course he was wearing rubber boots, and he scolded us the whole time. But it was nice of him to come and save us, although it was completely unnecessary. We didn't dare say that, of course.

We hurried away as fast as we could. He yelled after us that

he was sick and tired of Bullerby children, and next time we'd better leave his fence poles alone.

When we had gone quite a way I happened to look at Lars' satchel, and then I said, 'What have you done with Agda's shoes?'

Lars looked foolish. He'd left the shoes lying on the rock! He had put them down when he was fishing the cheese sandwich out of his bag. We all turned back because we thought it would be too bad to let him go back alone.

The shoes were there on the rock, all right, wrapped in newspaper. The shoemaker had taken away the fence poles, but, seeing it was so warm and sunny, Lars suggested that we should all take off our shoes and stockings and wade out. It wasn't really so terribly cold in the water.

We pretended the rock was a wrecked ship and we were pirates who had to climb aboard to save a valuable treasure – Agda's shoes. We pretended that there were lots of other pirates who were guarding the treasure on the wreck. We ran round in the water and shot at those pirates. Lars led us, and we climbed up on the wreck with knives between our teeth. Well, they were only sticks, but we pretended they were knives.

Finally we all got up on the rock. Lars swung Agda's shoes over his head and yelled, 'The loot is ours! Death to anyone who approaches us now!'

At that very second the shoemaker came back! He was the only one who approached us now. Poor man, I really felt sorry for him when he saw us, because then he understood that he had saved us in vain. He stood there a long while with his mouth wide open and didn't say a word. We sat there on the rock, as quietly as mice. Finally the shoemaker came to life.

'Get away from there!' he yelled. 'You'd better get away before I get hold of you!'

We jumped down, splashed ashore, picked up our shoes and stockings, and ran as fast as we could leaving Agda's shoes on the rock. The shoemaker yelled after us that it was certainly strange that we couldn't stay in Bullerby to make nuisances of ourselves there.

We walked home and didn't stop any more – except to look at a bird's nest Pip knew about in a tree. We climbed up, one at a time, and saw four little light blue eggs in it. Pip has eggs like that in his collection, but he is very careful about birds and birds' nests, so we looked very quietly.

This didn't take very long, but when I told Mother about it

she said, 'Now I'm beginning to understand why you can't possibly get home from school before five in the afternoon.'

Lars told Agda that she would get her shoes the next day. He had them in a very safe place, he said, and she didn't need to worry that they would get lost during the night. They were guarded by pirates and a very angry shoemaker.

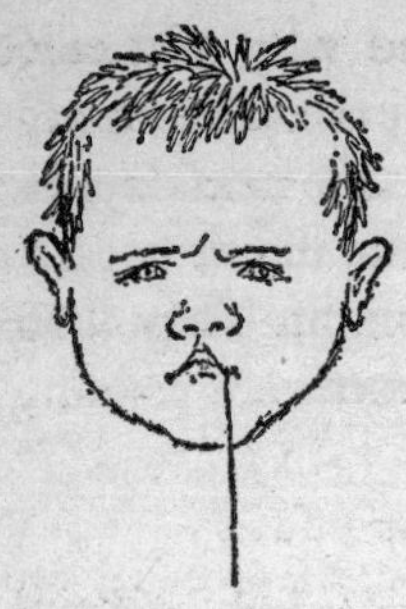

23. Olaf has a loose tooth

One day at school Miss Johnson said to Olaf, 'Why do you keep putting your fingers in your mouth?'

He looked very embarrassed, and then he said, 'I have a loose tooth.'

'Pull it out, then, when you get home,' said Miss Johnson. 'But not now. We have to do arithmetic now. Tomorrow we will all look at the gap where the tooth was.'

Olaf looked terrified, because he's frightened of pulling out a tooth no matter how loose it is. I don't like having a tooth pulled out either.

'My goodness, it won't hurt to pull out a little baby tooth like that,' Father says.

Maybe it doesn't hurt so much, but it's still horrid. Father gives us ten ore (about two pence in English money) for every tooth he pulls out. Of course, he only pulls out the ones that are loose, but that's quite enough, because I think you almost always have a loose tooth.

Pip isn't a bit afraid of pulling out his teeth, so he really shouldn't get ten ore when he pulls one. He just puts a strong thread round the tooth, gives it a jerk, and the tooth is out. Father always gives Pip ten ore because he is so brave.

But Olaf, poor thing, is more scared than I am of pulling teeth. He let us all feel his loose tooth when we were walking home from school. It was *really* loose.

'I can jerk that out for you in no time,' Pip said.

'You're not jerking out anything,' said Olaf. He hung his head all the way home and hardly said a word.

'Don't feel sad because you have a loose tooth,' I said. 'It's really nothing.' I said this because it was Olaf's tooth and not mine. It's only when you have a loose tooth yourself that it's scary.

'I know,' said Lars. 'When we get home you can tie a piece of strong thread round the tooth, and we'll tie the other end to the fence. I'll heat an iron skewer until it's red hot and swish it back and forth right in front of your nose. Then you'll be so scared that you'll jump backwards, and the tooth will pop out.'

'Iron skewers indeed!' Olaf said angrily. He didn't like that idea at all. But he did tie a piece of strong black thread round his tooth when we got home, so he could pull at it from time to time and make the tooth still looser. In some way he *had* to try to get rid of it, because Miss Johnson had said she was going to look at the gap the next day. I think that's what worried Olaf most. He had to have the tooth out by the next day, or Miss Johnson would know that he was afraid of pulling teeth.

Anna tried to console him. She said. 'Don't worry. Miss Johnson will probably forget all about your tooth by tomorrow.'

But Anna knew just as well as Olaf that Miss Johnson never forgets anything. Lars says she has a memory like an elephant's.

We played ball down on the road, as we usually do on spring evenings, and the whole time the long black thread hung out of Olaf's mouth. It looked so funny when he ran. At times he forgot the tooth, and the thread, and the whole bother; then he laughed and talked as usual. But all of a sudden he would look sad and peculiar and would tug at the thread and sigh.

'It's crazy! It's only fastened by a thin little piece of skin. For goodness' sake, pull it out!' one of us would say.

Olaf shuddered when he heard this. It's that last little piece of skin that's the worst.

When we got tired of playing ball, we went up to Grandpa's and told him that Olaf had a loose tooth.

'He has to pull it out tonight,' said Lars. 'Because Miss Johnson wants to see the gap tomorrow.'

Olaf almost started to cry when Lars said that.

'My, oh my,' said Grandpa. 'Speaking of teeth, I remember when I was a little boy –'

'Yes, Grandpa, tell about what happened when you were a little boy,' Anna said and climbed up in his lap.

Then Grandpa said that when he was a little boy he had a terrible toothache for a whole month, until finally he went to the blacksmith to have the tooth pulled. There were no dentists where he lived. The blacksmith took a big pair of pliers and pulled out Grandpa's tooth, and it hurt terribly. But after Grandpa went home he got an awful toothache again, because the blacksmith had pulled the wrong tooth. Grandpa then had a toothache for another month, but he didn't dare go back to the blacksmith, because it hurt so to have big molars pulled with a pair of pliers. But, finally, the tooth ached so badly that he *had* to go back. That time the blacksmith pulled the right tooth, but he almost lifted Grandpa out of the chair to do it because the tooth had such big roots and was so hard to get out.

'Poor Grandpa,' said Olaf.

I think that Olaf thought his own tooth was just as terrible to get out, although it didn't have any roots at all.

'Just imagine, Grandpa! You were once a little child afraid of having teeth pulled,' Anna said.

'My, oh my, that was a long time ago,' said Grandpa. 'Now I only have three teeth left, and they'll fall out by themselves any day.'

'So now you never have to be afraid again,' Anna said.

'No, my little friend. I never have to be afraid again,' said Grandpa.

Then he went to the corner cupboard and took out some barley-sugar for us. He gave us each a piece and said, 'You shouldn't eat barley-sugar. It'll give you a toothache. My, oh my!'

Then we said good night to Grandpa and left.

'Well, how about your tooth?' Lars said. 'Is it going to sit there until you get as old as Grandpa?'

Olaf got mad, and I don't blame him.

'Is it in your way?' he said. 'After all, it's my tooth, isn't it?'

'Yes, but when are you going to pull it out?' said Britta.

Olaf tugged a little at the thread and said, 'Tomorrow morning, maybe.'

Then he ran home, and Lars said, 'I feel sorry for Olaf. I know what I'll do. When he has gone to sleep I'm going to climb into his room and pull his tooth for him.'

'But do you really think you could do that?' we said.

'Of course,' he said. 'Lars Erikson, D.D.S., extracts teeth under complete anaesthesia.'

Then we said we wanted to come along and look. So we all ran up to Lars' and Pip's room and waited. We heard Olaf fussing around with something in his room at the other side of the linden tree.

Finally Lars called, 'Aren't you going to go to bed soon, Olaf?'

'Go to bed yourself,' Olaf said.

'Pip and I are already in bed,' Lars replied. We giggled quietly, because they were only lying on top of their beds and still had their clothes on.

'Aren't you sleepy, Olaf?' called Pip after a while.

'Yes, but you're making so much noise that I can't sleep,' said Olaf. So we thought he must have gone to bed by then.

'Turn out the light, Olaf,' Lars said.

'Turn out your own light,' Olaf answered, and Lars did. We sat in the dark and waited. After a while Olaf turned out his light.

'I hope he soon goes to sleep, because otherwise I shall,' said Anna, and yawned.

Just then we heard something rustle in the linden tree. It was Olaf on his way over to our house. Britta and Anna and I slipped quickly into the cupboard. Lars and Pip crept down in their beds and pulled the covers up to their chins.

'Pip,' said Olaf, while he climbed through the window. 'I'll probably be ill tomorrow, so I won't be able to go to school. In that case, you don't need to wait for me.'

'Ill! Why should you be ill?' Lars said. 'If you went to bed in decent time, you'd be as healthy as a fish.'

'I have a stomach ache,' said Olaf and crept back to his room.

I'm sure he had a stomach ache just because he was so nervous on account of his tooth.

We waited a long, long time, and finally we were so sleepy that we could hardly keep our eyes open.

'He must have gone to sleep by now,' Lars said at last. And

then he crept out into the linden tree. 'Are you awake, Olaf?' he said, as quietly as he could.

'No, I'm fast asleep,' said Olaf.

So we had to sit down and wait some more. Finally Lars said he was going over to see if Olaf had gone to sleep. If he hadn't, there was something wrong with him, and then Lars would go and get the doctor. So we all crept through the tree as quietly as we could. Lars had brought his flashlight, and he flashed it on Olaf's bed. There he lay, fast asleep, with the black thread trailing out of his mouth. Oh, I got so scared! What if it should hurt a lot, and Olaf started to cry! What would he say when he saw all of us standing there?

Lars took a firm grip on the thread and whispered, 'One, two, three, pull!'

And just as he said 'Pull!' he pulled – and there hung the tooth, dangling on the thread. Olaf didn't even wake up. He just mumbled in his sleep, 'I have a stomach ache.'

Pip tried to wake him up, but he couldn't. Lars said it was just as well, because now Olaf would think a ghost had been in his room and pulled his tooth. Lars tied the string to the light fixture in the ceiling, and there the tooth hung where it would be the first thing Olaf would see when he woke up. How happy he would be!

Olaf didn't have a stomach ache the next day. He was standing outside his gate and waiting for us, as usual. He laughed, so you could see a gap in his upper jaw.

'Was it you who did it, Lars?' he asked.

And then we told him that we had all been in his room. Olaf laughed still more when he heard what he had said in his sleep. He was so happy that he jumped up and down and kicked all the stones that lay in the road. Then he said, 'It really isn't too bad to have teeth pulled.'

'No, not under anaesthesia,' said Lars.

We decided that we'd all pull out one another's teeth at night. Well, I mean the loose ones, of course.

When we got to school, Olaf went right up to Miss Johnson, opened his mouth wide and said, 'Look, Miss Johnson. I pulled out my tooth!'

'I'm the one who did, to be more truthful,' Lars mumbled at his desk. But Miss Johnson didn't hear him.

24. The Chest of the Wizards

Olaf was as careful with the tooth that Lars had pulled out as if it had been a gold nugget. He kept it in a matchbox in his pocket, and from time to time he took it out and looked at it.

A couple of days later Pip had a loose tooth. It would have been the easiest thing in the world for him to pull it out himself. But Pip decided that he also wanted to have it pulled while he was sleeping. So he tied a long piece of strong string to his tooth just before he went to bed, and then he tied the other end to the knob of his door. The next morning when Agda came to wake up the boys and opened the door, the tooth popped out. Pip woke up even without Agda's having to shake him.

'It's strange how much fun you can have with teeth,' Pip said as we walked to school that day. He too had put his tooth in a matchbox, and he and Olaf were comparing teeth most of the way.

Lars was cross because he didn't have a tooth that had been pulled out. But he said, 'I wonder where I put that molar that the dentist in the village pulled last year.'

In the evening he looked through his drawers for the tooth and found many valuable things that he had thought were lost for ever. In a cigar box he found some chestnuts, several cartridge cases, a broken whistle, five broken tin soldiers, a broken fountain pen, a broken watch, and a broken flashlight, and then his molar. It was broken too. That was why it had been pulled.

Lars looked at all these broken things and said that he would mend them all sometime. Well, maybe not the tooth. He put it in a matchbox instead. All that evening Lars and Pip and Olaf went around rattling their matchboxes and looking superior. They didn't even want to play ball. So Britta and Anna and I played hopscotch and didn't pay any attention to them.

'I'm so tired of hearing about teeth now that I'm ready to pull out my own,' Britta said.

Just then the boys came along. They had been up in Lars' and Pip's room a long time, and they looked full of mischief.

'Don't ever tell the girls, whatever you do,' Lars said.

'I should say not! That would be a fine thing if *they* were told,' said Pip.

'We'll never tell them in a month of Sundays,' Olaf said.

We were so curious that we were ready to burst, but we didn't let on at all.

'Anna, it's your turn now,' I said.

We played hopscotch for dear life and pretended that we didn't even want to know whatever it was they were talking about.

The boys sat down by the side of the road and watched us.

'I hope you hid it really well,' Pip said to Lars.

'Don't worry,' Lars said. 'The Chest of the Wizards is something that you have to hide very carefully.'

'Yes, because otherwise the girls might find it,' Olaf said, 'and that would be a calamity.'

Lars made a face as if he couldn't think of a worse calamity.

'Olaf, please don't say such dreadful things!' he said. 'If the girls should find it – ye gods!'

'Lisa, it's your turn now,' Britta said.

We kept on playing hopscotch, pretending that we hadn't heard a word about the Chest of the Wizards.

Then the boys left. They walked down the road in a row, one behind the other. Anna pointed to them and whispered, 'There go the Wizards, haha!' And we laughed and laughed.

Lars turned round and said, 'It's good that you can keep your spirits up even though there are so many things in this world you know nothing about, you poor little things.'

Then we decided that we would look for the Chest of the Wizards. We guessed that it was just one of the boys' silly tricks, but we still wanted to find out where it was.

The boys had gone over to the pasture to ride Blossom, our black mare. So we rushed up to Lars' and Pip's room to hunt for the chest. We hunted and hunted. But it's not so easy to find the Chest of the Wizards when you don't even know what it looks like. We looked in the drawers and under the beds and on the shelves and in the fireplace and all over the attic. But we didn't find the Chest of the Wizards anywhere.

When we were right in the middle of our search, we heard the door to the attic open and the boys come stamping up. We moved fast like a flash of lightning. There are a lot of clothes hanging in the attic, so we hid behind them and stood very, very still – just as quiet as mice.

'Let's take it out and look at it again,' said Pip.

'First let's see where the girls are,' Lars answered. 'They're probably in Lisa's room, playing some silly old doll game.'

'No, if they were, we could hear them, couldn't we?' Olaf said. 'They're all probably over at North Farm. Come on, take out the Chest!'

We stood there and didn't dare move. I was afraid that I would have to sneeze or that I would start laughing. Then it looked as if Lars would walk right into me, and I thought, oh, now I'll die! But he stopped just in time and bent down and lifted up something; I couldn't see what. Anna poked me, and I poked her back.

'Wizards, do you swear never to give away the hiding place?' Lars asked.

'We swear never to let the unfaithful get hold of the Chest of the Wizards,' Pip and Olaf answered.

Of course, Britta and Anna and I were the 'unfaithful', so I poked Anna again.

'Yes, because if the unfaithful get hold of it, it will lose its secret powers,' said Lars.

I wanted so much to see this remarkable chest, but the boys were standing right in front of it. Finally Lars put it back where it had been under a loose board. Then they clumped down the stairs again.

Suddenly we came to life. As soon as the attic door was closed, we rushed out and pulled away the board. And there was the Chest of the Wizards! Well, what do you know – it was nothing but Lars' old cigar box! THE CHEST OF THE WIZARDS was written on the cover in large letters, and under that was drawn a skull and crossbones.

'Hurry and open it, Britta, so we can see what wonderful treasures are inside,' Anna said.

Britta did, and Anna and I craned our necks as far as we could, and all we saw were three white teeth – two little ones and a bigger one. That was all there was in the Chest of the Wizards.

'Sometimes I wonder if boys are quite right in their heads,' said Britta.

Then we saw Agda's bureau standing there in the attic. Mother had said that we were not, in any circumstances, to touch the bureau. But Agda is so kind. Sometimes she opens the bureau and shows me all the fine things she has in it. She has a little pink pincushion with lace, many pretty post cards with flowers on them, a perfume bottle that smells good, a bracelet made of gold, almost, and – well, there is so much that I can't tell you everything.

Last year when the dentist was in the village, he made Agda a set of new false teeth. He said that he had never seen such ugly false teeth as her old ones. It was too bad to have such ugly teeth when you looked so nice otherwise, he said.

But Agda didn't throw away the old teeth when she got the new ones. She said to me that perhaps she could use them on weekdays, or when the weather was bad, and save the new ones for Sundays.

'These teeth are certainly good enough to wear while I'm feeding pigs and milking cows,' she said.

But she soon got tired of the old teeth, because the new ones were so much prettier. Also Agda likes Oscar, our hired man, so she wants to look nice on weekdays too.

I knew that Agda kept the old teeth in the top drawer of her bureau, and that gave me an idea.

'I'll tell you what we can do,' I said to Britta and Anna. 'Let's put Agda's false teeth in the Chest of the Wizards. If the chest could get secret powers from three puny little baby teeth, think what it could get from a whole set!'

Britta and Anna thought that was a wonderful idea. It was much better than stealing the Chest of the Wizards, Britta said.

So we put Agda's teeth in the cigar box and put it back under the board. Then we went to look for the boys. They were way down the road, playing marbles. We sat down beside them in the road and watched them.

'Well, well, so the Wizards are playing marbles this beautiful evening,' said Britta.

They didn't answer. Lars had his hands full of marbles, and I said, 'The Chest of the Wizards would be a good place to keep the marbles in, I'll bet.'

They still didn't answer, but Lars gave a deep sigh. You could tell that he thought the unfaithful were even more stupid than usual.

'Can't you tell us about the Chest of the Wizards?' Anna asked and poked Lars in the ribs.

But Lars said it was nothing you could tell girls. The Chest of the Wizards was full of secret powers. Only the secret society that owned the chest was allowed to know where it was. 'Otherwise, it would lose its powers,' he said.

'The secret society – is that you and Pip and Olaf?' Britta asked.

Lars kept quiet and looked mysterious. But Britta and Anna and I started to laugh with all our might.

'I think they're peeved because they don't know where we keep the cigar – uh – the Chest of the Wizards,' Pip said.

'I bet it's in your cupboard,' said Britta slyly.

'I bet it isn't,' Pip said.

'Then I bet you it's under a loose board in the attic floor,' Anna said.

'I bet it isn't,' said the boys all at the same time. But they began to look worried! Their game of marbles got all confused.

'Let's go and look at your birds' eggs, Pip,' said Lars.

Did he really think we believed that's what they'd do? We knew for certain they were going to run and get the Chest of the Wizards.

'My birds' eggs! Why, you've seen them a hundred times,' said Pip. He is a little slow sometimes. Lars glared at him, and Pip finally understood.

'Oh, yes, of course, let's go and look at my birds' eggs,' he said.

The boys left us then – slowly, so that we wouldn't suspect anything. We didn't leave slowly, though. We ran over to Olaf's and told his mother that we were going to get something in his room. Then we rushed up the stairs and climbed through the linden tree to Lars' and Pip's room and ran into the attic and hid behind the clothes. We had just got there when the boys came clumping up the stairs.

'What do you think Anna meant about the attic floor?' Pip said. 'Does she know anything?'

'No,' said Lars. 'That was just something to say. But we'd better move the Chest of the Wizards to another hiding place just to be on the safe side.'

We couldn't see anything, because the boys were standing between us and the chest, but we heard Olaf say, 'Open it so I can look at my tooth.'

'I want to look at mine too,' said Pip.

'Wizards,' Lars said, 'what is hidden in this chest must never be seen by the unfaithful. Only by us.'

Then it got quiet, and we knew that Lars was lifting the lid. Then we heard a loud howl, so they must have caught sight of Agda's teeth. And we ran out from behind the clothes and laughed, and I said, 'Now I bet you have enough powers to last you a whole year.' Britta and Anna and I laughed again.

Lars threw Agda's teeth across the attic floor and said that girls should never have been born, because they always spoil everything.

Anna said, 'Lars, please make a miracle for us with the cigar box!'

'Do you want a beating?' said Lars.

Then Lars and Pip and Olaf threw away their teeth, and we all went out and played ball.

25. Lars captures musk oxen

There are two things I'm jealous of Britta and Anna about. The first is Grandpa. He says that with as few children as there are here in Bullerby, he can easily be a grandfather to all of us. But then Anna says, 'That may be, but you're still only my grandfather, really and truly. And Britta's too, of course!'

So when we're reading the paper to Grandpa, it's always Anna who sits on his lap, and he calls her 'my little friend'.

I can't understand how he can tell the difference between Anna and the rest of us when he's almost blind. But he can. Yet Anna isn't hairy like that Esau in the Bible. It was no trouble for Esau's daddy to tell his children apart when one of them was hairy and the other smooth. Grandpa is really clever, I think – especially since Anna isn't a bit hairy. Still, Grandpa is so very nice to all of us that it really doesn't make much difference that Anna is the one he calls 'my little friend'.

But Britta and Anna also have a lake of their own right next to their cow pasture. That's the other thing I'm jealous of. We go swimming there in the summer, and it has a lovely sandy beach.

On the other side of the lake there is no sandy beach, but there are high mountains. At least, *I* think they're high. We pretend that the mountains on the other side of the lake are the Rocky Mountains, and we row over there in the North Farm rowing-boat.

Lars says that a giant must have thrown all those big boulders and rocks around in our Rocky Mountains. That was a long time ago when there were no people, and no Bullerby. I'm glad that I didn't live then, when there was no Bullerby. Then we wouldn't have had anywhere to live. Lars says we would have had to live in the cave in the Rocky Mountains. There is one very big cave over there under a couple of huge boulders.

We always tie the rowing-boat to a certain pine when we get to the other side of the lake. Then we climb the mountains, but in our own special way. We have certain places where we can put our feet. This is necessary, because it is so hard to climb mountains. We have one crevice that we call the Nosescraper because it's so narrow that you almost always scrape your nose when you're going through it. But you *have* to go through the Nosescraper. There is no other way.

Then you go past a rock that juts away out, where you have to step on a very narrow ledge to get by. We call it the Armbreaker, because Lars says that once Pip fell down there and broke off his arm. Pip says that isn't so. Well, he did fall down, and he *nearly* broke his arm, but he certainly didn't break it off. But we call the rock the Armbreaker anyway.

The most dangerous part we call the Dead Man's Hand. If you fell down there, you'd have to be wheeled home in a wheelbarrow, Lars says, because you'd be dead.

When you've got past all those difficult places, you're almost up on top of the highest mountain. And then, if you walk a little way towards the forest, you come to the big cave we call the Rumble-hole.

One Sunday, just before the end of the school term last spring, we took a trip to the Rocky Mountains. We took a picnic lunch and told our mothers that we would probably be gone all day.

Lars tied the rowing-boat to the pine we always use, and then we started to climb. We talked about which was the most fun,

climbing mountains or climbing trees. And we all thought that it was just a little bit more fun climbing mountains.

After we had been through Nosescraper and Armbreaker and were climbing over Dead Man's Hand, I shivered a little because it was so exciting. Lars looked down into the depths and said, 'Everyone who intends to fall down here put up a hand or a foot!'

We certainly couldn't put up any hands or feet, because we needed them to hold on with, and, besides, nobody intended to fall down. Soon we were at the Rumble-hole.

We laid out our picnic lunch in a beautiful clearing in the woods right next to the Rumble-hole. You always get hungry right away when you're outdoors, so we all thought we might as well eat. We had flapjacks – about a hundred – with us, and jam, milk, fruit juice, sandwiches and biscuits.

Then we went into the cave. Lars said that perhaps people had lived there during the Stone Age. Goodness, they must have been cold in the winter! There were large openings between the rocks, where the snow could blow in.

Britta suggested that we should pretend we were Stone Age people. Lars thought that was a wonderful idea. He said that he and Pip and Olaf would go out to capture musk oxen, and that Britta and Anna and I should stay in the cave and keep the food warm.

Isn't that always the way? No matter what we play, the boys manage to do something that's fun while we stay and keep the food warm and things like that. Britta said we could take bunches of leaves to sweep the cave with, and then we could put some pretty birch branches in the cracks and make it homelike.

Lars said, 'Do whatever you want to, even if it's stupid! Come on, fellows! Let's go on out and capture musk oxen.'

But Pip was so full after eating more lunch than anyone else that he didn't feel like capturing musk oxen.

'Then you'll have to stay around the cave and beat the women and children,' Lars said. 'The main thing is for you to have something to do.'

'Just let him try,' said Britta.

But Pip was so full that he lay down in the grass in front of the cave. He stayed there all the time Lars and Olaf were hunting musk oxen and we were sweeping the cave.

Then Lars and Olaf came back and let out an awful howl – to

show that the hunt had been successful, Lars said. Lars said that it was a Stone Age howl, and that people howled that way when they were hunting musk oxen in the Stone Age. He bragged about how dangerous it was to hunt them, and said he had got a whole lot. We couldn't see any, though.

Then it started to rain, so we sat in the cave and had a nice time. The sky was so dark that we thought the weather probably wouldn't get sunny again that day. But then, all of a sudden, the sun came out from behind a cloud. So we left the cave and looked out over the lake. The sun shone on a big stone slab on an island in the middle of the lake, where we go swimming sometimes, and it looked very pretty.

Lars said, 'Let's row out there and have a swim.'

It hadn't been more than two days since we had asked Mother if we could go swimming soon, and she had said, 'No, it's too early. You'll have to wait a little longer.'

'Well, we *have* waited a little longer,' Lars said.

So we rowed over to the island. We undressed on the stone slab and had a race to see who could get into the water first. Pip won. His lunch must have sunk down by then.

But the water was so cold that we all came out very quickly. The first thing we saw when we came back to the stone slab was the angry ram from North Farm. He can't be kept in a pasture with the other sheep, because he jumps over all the fences and butts everyone he sees. In the spring he is usually kept out on the island by himself. It's an awful job to get him there. Uncle Erik and Father and Uncle Nils help one another to tie his feet with rope; then they put him in the rowing-boat, and Uncle Erik rows him out to the island and turns him loose.

We had forgotten about him and were very surprised when we came out of the water and saw the ram standing on the shore, staring at us. Ulrik is the ram's name.

'Oh, how awful!' said Anna. 'I'd forgotten all about Ulrik.'

I think Ulrik thinks it's terribly embarrassing to be tied up like that and put in a boat, with his wives and all the lambs looking on. Perhaps that's why he's usually so angry. Also, it's probably dull to walk round on that little island all alone.

Now he seemed even angrier than usual. He lowered his head and rushed towards us, and Olaf got such a push that he fell down. But he got up again and ran for dear life. So did the rest of us. Pip and Anna and Britta climbed up on a high stone; Olaf and I climbed up in a tree; and Lars hid behind a bush.

I yelled to Lars, 'All right, you're so clever at catching musk oxen! Here is one for you – almost. Show us now how you can catch him.'

And Anna and Britta cried, 'Yes, here comes the musk ox, Lars; catch him now!'

But Lars didn't dare answer, because he was standing behind the bush, and, if he spoke, Ulrik would know he was there.

Ulrik was furious because he couldn't get at us. He stood under the tree where Olaf and I were and butted it until the bark flew. When that didn't do any good, he went over to the high stone where Pip and Britta and Anna were. He stood below and glared at them as hard as he could.

'Go ahead and glare!' said Britta.

But then we started to wonder how we were going to get away from there. Ulrik didn't look as if he was going to leave.

'I do wish I had something to eat,' Pip said.

We had hidden what was left from lunch in the Rumblehole, and, now that Pip started talking about it, we were hungry too.

'Have you gone to sleep behind that bush?' Olaf called to Lars. Then Lars stuck his head out and looked round and tried to sneak over to the stone where Pip and Anna and Britta were.

But he should never have done that, because, when he did, Ulrik saw him.

He rushed towards Lars who started to run very fast. We all yelled, because it looked so terrible to see him running around in the juniper bushes, chased by Ulrik.

'Run, Lars, run!' Anna shouted.

'That's just what I'm doing,' Lars yelled.

Once Ulrik pushed Lars and he fell. Then we all yelled so loudly, it sounded like the Stone Age howl. I think the howl must have scared Ulrik a little.

Lars got up and ran on. Ulrik started after him, and we yelled still more, but it didn't help.

There is an old barn on the island with the roof falling in, so it isn't used any more. The door was wide open. Lars ran in there. Ulrik ran in too.

Then I started to cry and said, 'Oh, Ulrik will gore Lars to death there in the barn.'

But then, all of a sudden, we saw Lars come climbing up through the hole in the roof. He jumped down to the ground and ran to close the door of the barn.

'The musk ox is caught,' he said.

So, at last, we dared come down. And we all climbed up on the roof and looked down at Ulrik through the hole. Pip said, 'You nasty old ram, you!'

And I said, 'I hope Pontus never turns into a mean old ram like that!' Pontus was my pet lamb.

After that we had to go home. Lars told us all to get into the rowing-boat. He said he would open the door of the barn and then, before Ulrik understood what was going on, he would rush down and throw himself into the rowing-boat. He said that even if Ulrik was an angry old ram, you couldn't just leave him locked in the barn where he would starve to death.

We did as Lars said. We always do.

As we rowed away from the island, Ulrik stood on the shore and looked as if he felt very sad that we had left.

'Just tell me if there are any more musk oxen that you want captured,' Lars said, looking pleased with himself.

But we didn't want any more musk oxen captured that day. We were so tired and hungry we just wanted to get home.

'I'll see if Mother has anything to eat,' Pip said.

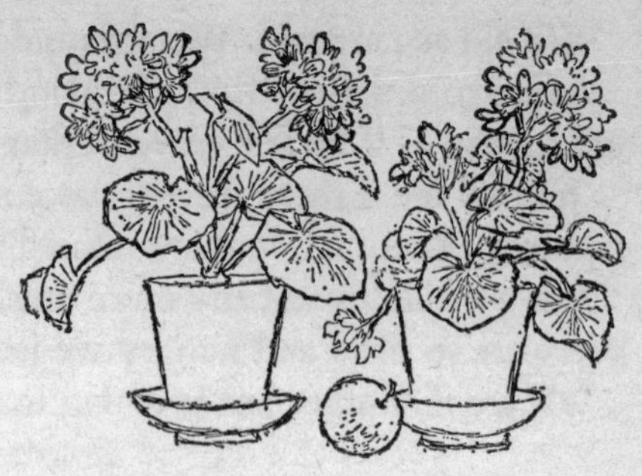

26. Midsummer in Bullerby

And now I want to tell you about what we did on Midsummer Eve, the twenty-third of June. In the South Farm meadow we had a Midsummer pole. (We always have one in Sweden.) Everybody in the whole village helped to make it.

First we rode way out into the forest in our wagon to pick leaves that we were going to use. Father drove, and even Kerstin was allowed to come along. She was so happy that she laughed and laughed. Olaf gave her a little branch to hold in her hand, and she sat and waved it back and forth. And Olaf sang this old song for her:

'Kerstin had a little gold coach
In which she was going to ride;
A little gold whip she held in the air
And smiled on the world with pride . . .'

All the rest of us sang too. Agda had come along to help us pick leaves and she sang:

'Now it is summer;
Now there is sunshine;
Now there are flowers and leaves . . .'

When we came home from the forest, Agda, Britta, Anna, and I picked a big bunch of lilacs from the bushes behind our woodshed.

Then we took them over to the South Farm meadow, where Oscar and Kalle had already cut the pole. We tied the leaves all round the pole and hung two big wreaths of lilacs from the crossbar at the top. Then we raised the pole and danced round it.

Uncle Erik, Anna's father, plays the accordion well, and he played a lot of gay tunes for us all to dance to – all except Grandpa and Kerstin. Grandpa sat in a chair and Kerstin sat in his lap at first. But she couldn't stop pulling his beard, so her daddy put her up on his shoulders. In that way, Kerstin could dance with us too.

Poor Grandpa couldn't dance, but I don't think he was sorry. He just said, 'My, oh my, it seems longer ago than yesterday that I danced round a Midsummer pole!'

Then we all sat down in the grass and drank coffee that Mother and Aunt Greta and Aunt Lisa had made. We had buns and cakes too. Grandpa drank three cups of coffee, because that's something he really likes.

'Coffee is something I have to have,' he says.

I don't like it at all, but when you drink it while sitting in the grass at Midsummer, it tastes much better than usual.

We played 'The last pair out' and a lot of other games. It's such fun when the mothers and fathers play with us. It would probably not be so much fun if we had to play with them every

day, but when it's Midsummer, I think they should be allowed to play too.

Svipp ran round and barked while we played. I think he thought it was fun too.

We were allowed to stay up just as long as we wanted to that evening. Agda said if you climbed over nine fences before you went to bed, and if you picked nine kinds of flowers and put them under your pillow, you'd dream at night about the one you would marry.

Britta and Anna and I thought it would be lots of fun to climb over nine fences, although we already know who we are going to marry. I'm going to marry Olaf, and Britta and Anna are going to marry Lars and Pip.

'Are you going to climb over nine fences?' Lars said to Britta. 'Well, go ahead, by all means. But please dream about someone else and not me. Not that I'm superstitious, but it *might* help.'

'Yes, let's hope you don't dream about us,' Pip said.

'Yes, let's *certainly* hope so,' Olaf said.

The boys are stupid and don't want to marry us.

Agda said that you had to be very quiet while you climbed over the fences. You couldn't laugh or talk at all the whole time.

'If you can't talk the whole time, Lisa,' Lars said, 'then you might just as well go to bed.'

'Why?' I said.

'Because you can't climb nine fences in two minutes, and you've never been quiet longer than that in your life – except the time you had the mumps, of course.'

We didn't pay any attention to the boys but just started climbing. We began with the fence round the South Farm meadow and came into the birch woods behind it.

It's strange in the woods when it's dark. Well, it wasn't perfectly dark, just rather twilightish and still. It was very quiet, because the birds had stopped chirping, and it smelled so good because of all the trees and flowers. We each picked a flower when we had climbed over the first fence.

There is one thing that I don't understand and that's why you always get the giggles when you know that you're not supposed to laugh. As soon as we had climbed over the first fence, we started.

The boys came climbing after us just to tease us and make us laugh.

'Don't step in the mud puddle,' Pip said to Anna.

'There's no puddle –' Anna said. But then she remembered that she wasn't supposed to talk. Then Britta and Anna and I giggled, and the boys laughed out loud.

'You can't giggle like that,' Lars said. 'Remember that you're not supposed to laugh.'

Then we giggled still more. And the boys ran round us and pulled our hair and pinched our arms to make us laugh. We couldn't say anything because we weren't supposed to talk.

'Ubbelibubbelimuck,' Lars said.

It wasn't a bit funny, really, but Britta and Anna and I couldn't keep from laughing. I stuffed my handkerchief in my mouth, but that didn't help; my laughter came chirping out all the same. But when we had climbed over the ninth fence, and

picked our ninth flower, we stopped laughing and were just mad at the boys for spoiling everything for us.

But even though I was angry with the boys I put the flowers under my pillow. I had a buttercup and a coltsfoot and a bluebell and a daisy and an almond flower and a rockrose and a violet and two other flowers that I don't know the names of. I didn't dream anything at all that night, and I'm certain that it was because those silly boys had made us laugh.

But I'm going to marry Olaf anyway, so there!

27. Nursemaids

One day last summer the pastor in the big village invited everyone in Bullerby to a large birthday party. Well, he didn't invite the children, but Mother and Father and Uncle Erik were invited – and all the other grown-ups, even Grandpa. Aunt Lisa felt badly, because she didn't think that she could go because of Kerstin, her little girl. Then Anna and I said we could look after her. We were going to be nursemaids when we grew up, so it would be a good thing if we started practising right away.

'But do you have to practise on my sister?' Olaf said.

He would have liked to look after Kerstin himself, but he had to milk the South Farm cows and feed the pigs and chickens while his mother and father were at the party. Britta would have liked to help too, but she was in bed with a terrible cold.

Aunt Lisa was very happy when we told her what we wanted to do, but Anna and I were even happier. I pinched Anna's arm and said, 'Won't it be fun?'

And Anna pinched me back and said, 'I wish they'd hurry and leave soon, so we could start.'

But it always takes a terribly long time for people to get ready for a party – except Grandpa. He was ready at six o'clock in the morning, although they weren't supposed to leave until ten. He was all dressed up in his black Sunday suit and his best white shirt.

As soon as Uncle Erik had hitched up the horses, Grandpa

went to the North Farm wagon and sat down to wait. This was even before Aunt Greta had started to put on her party dress.

Aunt Lisa kept on giving us all sorts of instructions until the very last minute, and then Father and Uncle Nils and Uncle Erik smacked their horses, and they all drove off.

Aunt Lisa had said that we should let Kerstin be outdoors as much as possible, because she was the least trouble there. At noon she should have her lunch which was all ready to heat; after that, she should take a nap for a couple of hours.

'Won't that be fun!' Anna said.

'Yes,' I said. 'I'm sure I'm going to be a nursemaid when I grow up.'

'Me too,' said Anna. 'It's really easy to take care of children. All you have to do is remember to speak softly and kindly to them. Then they mind you. I read that in the newspaper the other day.'

'Yes, of course,' I said.

'But you know there are people who yell at their children,' Anna said. 'And those children never mind their parents, and they grow up to be real little horrors. It said that in the paper.'

'Who would want to yell at such a sweet little thing?' I said, and tickled Kerstin's foot.

Kerstin sat on a blanket on the lawn and looked happy. She has a round little forehead, and her eyes are bright blue. In her mouth she has four teeth upstairs and four down, which look just like grains of rice when she laughs. The only thing she can say is 'hi, hi', and she says that almost all the time. Perhaps she means different things every time, but you never know.

Sometimes Kerstin rides in a wooden cart.

'How about taking her for a ride?' Anna suggested.

So we did.

'Come here, Kerstin, dear,' Anna said and put her down in the cart. 'Now we are going to go for a little ride.'

She spoke very softly and kindly, just the way you should to little children.

'There now, aren't you nice and comfy?' she said.

But Kerstin didn't think so at all. She started to stand straight up in the cart and jump up and down and say 'hi, hi', but, of course, we couldn't let her do that.

'I think we'd better tie her down,' I said. So we did – with a heavy piece of cord. But then Kerstin started to howl so loudly you could hear it a mile away.

Olaf came running from the barn and said, 'What are you doing to my little sister?'

'Nothing, stupid,' I said. 'We are just speaking softly and kindly to her!'

'Well, that's all right,' Olaf said. 'But also you'd better let her do what she likes, so she won't cry.'

We thought Olaf should know how his sister should be taken care of, so we let Kerstin stand up in the cart and say 'hi, hi', all she wanted. I would pull the cart while Anna ran along beside Kerstin to catch her every time she fell. Then we came to a deep ditch, and when Kerstin saw it, she climbed out of the cart.

'Let's see what she is going to do,' Anna said.

Well, she showed us all right! There's something odd about little children. You think that their legs are too short to run very fast, but that's where you're wrong. A little child can run as fast as a rabbit if he tries to. At least, Kerstin can. She said 'hi, hi', and ran right down into the ditch before we had time to wink an eye. There she stumbled and fell on her head in the water.

It's true that Olaf had said we should let her do what she

wanted to, and she wanted to lie in the ditch, but we still thought we'd better pull her out. She was sopping wet and yelling at the top of her voice. She scowled at us as if it had been our fault that she had fallen in. But we spoke softly and kindly to her and put her back in the cart. We pulled her home to get some dry clothes, and she yelled the whole time. Olaf was furious when he saw how Kerstin looked.

'What do you think you're doing anyway?' he shouted. 'Did you try to drown her?'

Then Anna said that he should speak softly and kindly to us, because we were children too – except we were big ones, of course.

But Kerstin went over and threw her arms round Olaf's legs and cried, so Anna and I felt just as if we *had* tried to drown her.

Olaf helped us find some clean clothes for Kerstin. Then he had to go to the barn again.

We put Kerstin's best dress on, because Olaf hadn't been able to find any other. It was very pretty – white with tiny little tucks and ruffles.

'You have to be very careful of this dress,' I said to Kerstin, but it was quite evident that she didn't understand what I said, because she ran right over to the stove and got a big soot-spot right in the middle of her dress. 'Hi, hi,' she said.

We brushed it off as well as we could, but it was impossible to get much of it off. Kerstin laughed when we brushed her. She probably thought that we were playing a game.

'It's twelve o'clock,' Anna said all of a sudden. 'It's time for Kerstin to have her lunch.'

We hurried to heat up her spinach in a saucepan on the stove. I took Kerstin on my lap, and Anna fed her. She ate very well and opened her mouth so nicely that Anna said, 'She really is an awfully nice little girl.'

Then Kerstin said 'hi, hi', and hit the spoon down on the table. All the spinach flew into my eyes.

Anna laughed until she almost dropped the plate, and I got furious with her. Kerstin laughed too, but she probably didn't know why Anna was laughing. She must think that it's quite natural for people to have spinach between the eyes.

Then all of a sudden, when she didn't want to eat any more, she closed her mouth tight and hit the spoon on the table again and again so that more than half of her spinach got on her dress. We gave her some fruit juice to drink from a cup, and more than half of that got on her dress too.

After that, the beautiful dress wasn't white any longer but green and red with just a little bit of white in certain spots.

'There's one thing I'm happy about,' Anna said, 'and that is that it's time for Kerstin to take a nap now.'

'Yes, that's one thing I'm happy about too,' I said.

And then we took off all of Kerstin's clothes again and put on her pyjamas. When we had finally finished, we were worn out.

'We're the ones who need to take a nap, not Kerstin,' I said to Anna.

But we put Kerstin in her cot and went out of the nursery and closed the door.

Then Kerstin started howling as loudly as she could. We tried to pretend that we didn't hear her, but she cried louder and louder until finally Anna stuck her head through the door and said, 'Be quiet, you naughty girl!'

Of course we knew that you should speak softly and kindly to little children, but sometimes you just can't. But what the paper said was probably right: that children become regular little horrors when you yell at them. At least Kerstin did. She cried louder than ever. Then we both went into her room.

She was happy as soon as she saw us and stood up in her cot; she jumped up and down and said 'hi, hi', the whole time we were in there. And she stuck her little hand out between the bars and patted me. When I leaned over the cot, she laid her cheek against mine.

'She's awfully sweet, even if she *is* naughty,' I said.

Then Kerstin bit my cheek, so I had a mark for two days.

We laid her down in the cot and tried to tuck the blanket around her, but she kicked it off. When she had kicked it off ten times, we didn't pay any more attention to her. We just said, 'Sleep well now, dear,' very softly and kindly. Then we went out and closed the door. Right away she started howling again.

'Enough is enough,' Anna said. 'Let her yell!'

We sat down at the kitchen table and tried to talk, but we couldn't because Kerstin yelled louder and louder and louder. Sometimes she was quiet for a couple of seconds but that was only when she took a breath for the next howl.

'Perhaps she has an ache somewhere,' I said.

'Goodness, what if she has a stomach ache,' Anna said. 'It could be appendicitis, or something.'

So we *ran* into Kerstin's room. She stood up in bed, and her eyes were filled with tears, but as soon as she saw us, she said 'hi, hi', and started to jump up and down and laugh.

'That child hasn't a stomach ache or any other kind of ache,' Anna said. 'Come on, let's go!'

So we closed the door and sat down by the kitchen table again, listening to Kerstin howl louder and louder. Finally she was quiet.

'Oh, how wonderful,' I said. 'She has gone to sleep at last.'

Anna and I took out Olaf's Old Maid game and sat down and played Old Maid, and it was very nice.

'Babies should stay in bed all the time. Then, at least, you know where they are,' Anna said.

Then we heard a strange noise from the nursery. It sounded like a little happy mumble, the kind of sound that children make when they are doing something pleasant.

'No, now this is going too far,' I said. 'It can't be possible that she's *still* awake!'

We tiptoed up and peeped carefully through the keyhole. We could see Kerstin's cot, but we couldn't see Kerstin. Her cot was empty. We rushed into the nursery. And guess where Kerstin was?

She was sitting in the open fireplace that had been beautifully whitewashed for the summer. I mean it *had* been beautiful, before Kerstin got there. It wasn't exactly beautiful any longer,

because Kerstin was sitting in the middle of it with a jar of shoe polish in her hand. She was black with shoe polish from head to toe.

She had shoe polish in her hair and shoe polish all over her face and shoe polish on her hands and on her pyjamas and on her feet, and all of the fireplace was decorated with shoe polish. Probably Uncle Nils had stood by the fireplace to polish his shoes before the party and then hadn't put the cover back on the jar.

'Hi, hi,' Kerstin said when she saw us.

'Did it say in the paper whether you could spank little children?' I said.

'I don't remember,' Anna said.

Then Kerstin stood up and ran towards Anna, and Anna yelled even louder than she did, '*Don't touch me, you naughty girl!*'

Kerstin did touch her. Anna grabbed her hands but still got shoe polish all over herself. Then I laughed just as hard at Anna as she had at me when I had got the spinach between my eyes.

'Aunt Lisa won't know her child when she sees her,' I said, when I had stopped laughing.

We didn't know how to wash off shoe polish, so we decided to ask Britta. Anna, who was already smeared, would stay and hold Kerstin while I went to ask her.

When I told Britta what Kerstin had done, she said, 'Well, you're a fine pair of nursemaids!' Then she blew her nose and turned towards the wall and said that she was ill and didn't know how you washed off shoe polish.

In the meantime Olaf had come from the barn, and he went absolutely wild when he saw Kerstin.

'Are you out of your minds?' he yelled. 'Have you painted her black?'

We tried to explain to him that it wasn't our fault. But Olaf was furious and said that there should be a law against people like us becoming nursemaids, and, in any case, we'd have to get another child to practise on.

But we all helped one another fill a tub with warm water. Then we carried it out on the lawn and led Kerstin out to it.

When she walked across the floor, she left funny little black footprints.

We put her in the tub and scrubbed her thoroughly from top to toe. We washed her hair too. She got a little soap in her eyes, and then she yelled so loudly you could hear it all over Bullerby. Lars and Pip came running and asked if we were slaughtering pigs.

'No,' Olaf said, 'It's just these two fine nursemaids who are practising.'

We couldn't get the shoe polish really off, and when we had finished scrubbing and drying Kerstin, she was a peculiar grey colour all over. But she was happy none the less. She ran around on the lawn, stark naked, and yelled 'hi, hi', and laughed so you could see every tooth in her mouth. Olaf said, 'Isn't she a darling baby?'

We thought that the grey colour would probably wear off in time so the pink child who was underneath would show up again. It would be around Christmas time, Lars thought.

Afterwards Olaf put Kerstin to bed. She didn't say boo, just stuck her thumb in her mouth and went to sleep.

'That's the way to take care of children,' Olaf said. Then he went to feed the pigs.

Anna and I sat down on the kitchen steps to rest.

'Poor Aunt Lisa, who has it like this every day,' I said.

'Do you know what I think?' Anna said. 'I think all that in the paper was a lie, because it doesn't make any difference *how* you talk to little children. Whether you talk softly and kindly or yell at them, they still do exactly as they please.'

After that we were quiet a while.

'Anna, are you going to be a nursemaid when you grow up?' I said finally.

'Perhaps,' Anna said. But then she looked thoughtful and stared out over the barn roof and said, 'Well, I really don't know.'

28. The Cherry Company

Anna may be right after all when she says that we have the most fun in the summer. But I like to go to school too, and when Miss Johnson says good-bye to us on the last day I almost cry, because I know that I won't see her for such a long time. But I soon forget about this, because it's so wonderful to have summer holidays.

The first evening of our summer holiday we usually go fishing at the North Farm lake. There's hardly anything that feels as summery as fishing. We make the rods ourselves of hazel branches, but we get lines and floats and sinkers and hooks from the store at the big village.

Lars calls the night we finish school the Big Fishing Night. There is a rock that's not too big and not too small where we sit to fish. It's called the Perch Rock, Anna says, because you never catch any perch there. The only thing you catch is mosquito bites. But Pip *did* catch a big perch the last time we were there. Britta caught two small roaches.

Later, Anna and I sat on our kitchen steps and counted mosquito bites. I had fourteen on my right leg and five on my left. Anna had nine on each leg.

'You could use that for a problem in arithmetic,' Anna said. 'Let's write it down for Miss Johnson: "If Lisa has fourteen mosquito bites on one leg and five on the other, and Anna has nine on each leg, who has the most mosquito bites, and how many do they have altogether?" '

But suddenly we remembered that it was the summer

holiday – and it's silly to do arithmetic then. So we just scratched our bites and had fun until bedtime.

How wonderful it is to have summer holidays! One thing we did last summer was to organize a Cherry Company.

We have lots of cherry trees in our garden and in Anna's and Britta's garden. In Olaf's garden there aren't any, at least none that are any good. The South Farm garden has, instead, a tree with fine August pears, and two trees with little delicious yellow plums.

The largest cherry tree in the world, I think, is outside Grandpa's window. We call it 'Grandpa's cherry tree'. Its branches droop down almost to the ground, and every summer it's full of big cherries.

Grandpa says that we may eat as many as we want to, but we mustn't pick the cherries from the lowest branches because they are for Kerstin. Grandpa wants Kerstin to be able to pick them herself. And she can too, although she's very little. But Olaf has to watch her, or she'll swallow the stones too. We do as Grandpa says and don't pick any cherries from Kerstin's branches.

It is very easy for us to climb up in the tree and pick there. There are many good branches and many forks in the branches where you can sit and eat all you want. Our stomachs hurt a little every year during the cherry season. After the cherries are all gone, we don't have stomach aches any more until the plums get ripe.

Mother always dries the cherries and keeps them through the winter. She puts them on a baking sheet in the oven when it's just barely warm. Then the cherries get dry and wrinkled and you can save them to make fruit soup during the winter.

Lars and Pip and I each have a cherry tree of our own. This year they all had an unbelievable amount of cherries.

Although Britta and Anna and Olaf helped us, we couldn't possibly eat all the cherries on our trees. One day Lars was going to dry some, and he filled a whole baking sheet and put it in the oven. Then he went swimming and forgot all about his cherries. When he looked at them again they had turned into tiny black, burned seeds.

'That's not the right way to treat cherries,' he said.

Then one night we were up in Grandpa's room, reading the paper, and it said that in Stockholm cherries cost two crowns a quart. Lars was very upset to think that he didn't have his cherry tree in Stockholm.

'Then I'd sell my cherries on a street corner and become as rich as the king,' he said.

We tried to work out how much money we would earn if only our cherry trees were in Stockholm. It was so much that Lars turned quite pale when he thought about it.

'If only I had the North Farm lake in the Sahara Desert, I could sell water for two crowns a quart also,' said Britta, who thought Lars was silly.

I think Lars lay awake that night and thought and thought about getting two crowns a quart for cherries in Stockholm, because the next day he said he was going to open a cherry stall on the highway that runs on the other side of the big village. There are so many cars passing there.

'And who knows, some crazy Stockholmers might even come by,' he said.

Pip and I said we wanted to sell our cherries too. So we made a company that we called the Cherry Company. We let Britta and Anna and Olaf be members too, because they helped us to pick our cherries although they did not have any trees of their own.

We got up at five o'clock one morning and started picking.

By eight o'clock we had three large baskets of cherries. Then we all ate a lot of oatmeal, so that we'd be able to go without food for a long while, and started out towards the big village. We went by Uncle Emil's shop and bought many brown paper bags with some money we had borrowed from Pip.

'What do you think you're going to do now?' Uncle Emil asked.

'We're going to sell cherries,' Lars said.

We had left Olaf watching the baskets on the steps outside the shop.

'Cherries, now that's something I like,' Uncle Emil said. 'Perhaps you'll sell some to me?'

Wasn't that good? Uncle Emil measured out two quarts for himself and gave us two crowns for them. He said that a crown a quart was the price for cherries in these parts and that it was a good thing for us to know.

Pip got back the money we had borrowed from his piggy bank, and we still had some left. Uncle Emil gave us some toffee. When Olaf saw this through the glass in the door, he came rushing into the store as if he had been attacked by a swarm of bees. When he had got his piece of toffee, he rushed out again almost as fast.

We thanked Uncle Emil, and when we got outside, we saw that Olaf was picking up some cherries that he had spilled in the grass.

'What are you *doing*?' Lars said angrily.

'I – I'm just polishing your cherries,' Olaf said and sounded scared.

But he had only spilled a few, so it didn't matter.

The highway runs very close to the big village. In the autumn and winter you see practically nothing on it but lorries.

In the summer, though, many cars pass by, because people want to see how beautiful the scenery is here.

'How can they see anything at all, when they drive so fast?' said Lars as the first car zoomed past.

We had made a big sign that said CHERRIES, and we held it up every time a car came by. But the cars just drove on. Lars said the people in them probably thought it said DRIVE CAREFULLY, and that was why they rushed by. But Pip thought it was fun to see the cars going so fast. He almost forgot the cherries. His eyes were perfectly round from staring, and he knew the make of every car.

Lars got furious because the cars didn't stop and he said, 'I'll teach them!'

So when the next car started coming he jumped out in the middle of the road and held up the sign. He didn't jump out of the way until the very last minute before he would have been run over.

The car stopped with a dreadful squealing of brakes, and a man got out and grabbed Lars by the arm. He said he'd give him a beating that he'd never forget.

'Don't you ever try anything like that again,' he said.

Lars promised not to do it again, and then, do you know, the man bought a quart of cherries from us before he left.

There was an awful lot of dust on the road. We had covered the cherries with paper, which was probably a good thing, but we couldn't very well cover ourselves. And every time a car drove by, a whole cloud of dust fell on us.

'What awful dust!' I said.

Lars asked why I had said that. 'Why don't you say "what awful sunshine!" or "what awful birdsong?" ' he wondered. Anyway who said we had to like sunshine and not like dust? So we decided we would like the dust. When the next car went by, and all the dust whirled round us so that we could hardly see each other, Lars said, 'What wonderful dust!'

And Britta said, 'Yes there's so much lovely dust on this road – really lovely!'

And Pip said, 'I only wish there was a lot more dust.'

He didn't have to wait long for his wish to come true. A big lorry came thundering by, and I didn't know there was so much dust in the whole world as whirled up behind the lorry. Anna stood right in the middle of it and stretched her arms in the air and said, 'What wonderful, wonderful dust!'

But then she started to cough, so she couldn't say anything

more. When the dust had settled a little we looked at each other; all of us were grey-black.

Although the dust was wonderful, we thought it was a shame that no cars wanted to stop. But finally Lars discovered that we were standing at a stupid place – right in the middle of a straight stretch where the cars were going at high speed. We should move to a curve in the road, he said.

So we placed ourselves a little farther away where there were two bends in the road, one just after the other. Then we got the idea of standing in a long row along the side of the road and holding one another by the hand and swinging our arms when a car approached.

'This'll do the trick!' Lars said.

And it did. Almost every car stopped. In the first car that came there were a mother and father and four children, and all the children cried for cherries.

Their father bought three quarts, and their mother said, 'Wasn't it lucky we found you! We were so hungry and thirsty!'

They bought the little black cherries from my tree. The father told us that they were going far, far away – all the way to a foreign country.

'Isn't it strange,' I said, 'that my cherries are going abroad while I am staying right here in Bullerby?'

But Lars said, 'Don't be silly! The children will have eaten the cherries long before they get to the foreign country.'

But I said, 'Even if the cherries were in the tummies of those children, they would go abroad anyway.'

Finally we had sold every cherry. We had thirty crowns in the cigar box that we had taken along to keep the money in. Thirty crowns was a terrific lot of money! We divided it so that we got five crowns each.

'And now that you haven't any cherries left, you may eat as many as you like in our garden,' Britta said.

'And I'll give you plums, as soon as they're ripe,' Olaf said when he got his five crowns.

So you have to admit that the money was fairly divided.

On our way home we went to the confectioner's shop in the big village and ate a piece of cake each and drank fizzy lemonade. We could afford to buy that much. We decided to save the rest of the money.

When we came home and Mother caught sight of Lars and Pip and me, she threw up her hands and said she had never seen such a dirty cherry company. She wanted us to go out to the laundry room and wash. But just then Anna came and cried, 'What luck! The Finnish bath is heated!'

Britta and Anna had a Finnish bath down by the lake. We took along clean clothes and ran through the cow pasture, as fast as we could.

In the lake we washed off all the wonderful dust. Then we sat in the Finnish bath to sweat. We decided we were going to make a plum company too, a little later.

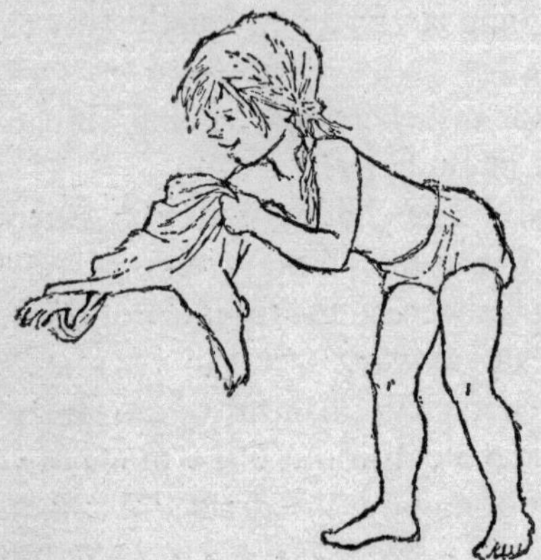

It's awfully hot in the Finnish bath, and finally we were so warm that we almost burst. Then we ran out and cooled off in the lake.

How wonderful it felt! We splashed water on each other and swam and dived. And when we came up there was no wonderful dust left, not even in our hair.

The weather was so beautiful. We sat on the shore and sunbathed. Lars said, 'What awful sunshine!'

And then Olaf laughed and said, 'What awful birdsong!'

29. Anna and I make people happy

One day at school Miss Johnson said we should always try to make other people happy. We should never do anything that would make anyone feel sad, she said. Well, that same afternoon Anna and I sat on our back stairs talking, and we decided to start making people happy right away.

The trouble was that we didn't quite know how to go about it. We decided to start with Agda, so we went into the kitchen, where she was scrubbing the floor.

'Don't step on the floor when it's wet,' she said hastily.

'Agda,' I said, 'can you tell me something that we could do to make you happy?'

'Yes, if you would get out of the kitchen while I'm scrubbing the floor, I should be very happy,' said Agda.

We went outside again. It wasn't much fun to make people happy that way. Anyway, I don't think that's what Miss Johnson meant.

Mother was in the orchard, picking apples. I walked over and said, 'Mother, tell me something I can do to make you happy.'

'I'm already happy,' Mother said.

That was too bad, but I didn't want to give up, so I said, 'But couldn't I do something to make you even happier?'

'You don't have to do anything except keep right on being my good little girl,' said Mother. 'Then I'll be quite happy enough.'

So I went back to Anna, and I said that Miss Johnson probably had no idea how hard it was to find someone to make happy.

'I know, let's try Grandpa,' Anna said.

So we went to Grandpa's.

'Are my little friends coming to see me?' said Grandpa. 'That makes me very happy!'

Wasn't that a shame! We had hardly come inside the door, and Grandpa was already happy. There was nothing left for us to do.

'No, Grandpa,' said Anna. 'Don't tell us that you're *already* happy. We want to do something to *make* you happy. You have to help us think of something, because Miss Johnson says we have to make other people happy.'

'You could perhaps read the paper to me. That would make me happy,' said Grandpa.

'Well, yes, but we do that so often that there's nothing special about it.'

All of a sudden Anna said, 'Grandpa, you hardly ever leave this room. Wouldn't you be awfully happy if we took you for a walk?'

Grandpa didn't look very happy at the suggestion, but he promised to go with us. Anna and I walked on either side of Grandpa and led him, because he can't see where he's going. We took him all round Bullerby and talked and told him things the whole time.

The wind had started to blow, and it was raining a little, but we didn't mind because we were determined to make Grandpa happy.

As we were walking along Grandpa said, 'Don't you think we've walked enough now? I'd like to go to bed.'

We led Grandpa back to his room. He undressed right away and crept into his bed, although it wasn't night yet. Anna tucked him in. He looked a little tired.

Before we left, Anna said, 'Grandpa, what's the nicest thing that's happened to you all day?'

We both thought that he'd say that the walk had been the nicest thing. But Grandpa said, 'The nicest thing that's happened to me today – well, snuggling down in my nice warm bed. I feel very tired.'

Afterwards Anna and I had to do our homework, so we didn't have time to make any more people happy that day. The next day we still weren't quite sure that we knew the right way to make people happy, so we decided to ask Miss Johnson about it.

Miss Johnson told us that often very little was needed. You

could perhaps sing a song for someone who was ill and alone, or give a flower to someone who never got flowers, or speak kindly to someone who felt bashful and out of things.

Anna and I decided to try again. That afternoon I heard Agda tell Mother that Ingrid was ill. She lives by herself in a little house at the edge of the woods. I ran over to Anna right away and said, 'What luck! Ingrid is ill. Come on, let's go over there and sing to her!'

Ingrid seemed quite pleased to see us, but she probably wondered why we didn't bring her anything in a basket, because we usually do.

'Do you want us to sing something for you?' I asked.

'Sing?' said Ingrid, and looked surprised. 'Why?'

'To make you happy,' said Anna.

'All right, go ahead,' said Ingrid.

We started with 'Oh, Susannah', and then we sang 'The Farmer in the Dell', all seven verses of it.

Ingrid didn't look any happier than she had when we started. So then we sang 'Little Miss Muffet', and 'The Old Woman Who Lived in a Shoe', and 'Mary Had a Little Lamb', and a couple more songs, but Ingrid still didn't look the least bit happier.

We were beginning to get hoarse but we weren't going to stop singing until we had made her very happy.

We were just starting 'Little Bo-Peep' when Ingrid climbed out of bed and said, 'You can stay and sing as much as you like, but I'm going to take a little walk.'

Anna and I didn't think it was worth trying any longer, so we said good-bye to Ingrid.

'Perhaps it would work better to give flowers to someone who never gets flowers,' said Anna.

We were just wondering whom we could find to give

flowers to when we saw Oscar, the farm hand, walking into the barn. We ran after him, and I said, 'Oscar, have you ever had any flowers given to you?'

'I should think not. I'm not dead yet, am I?' said Oscar.

Poor thing, he probably thought you only had flowers at your funeral. Anna looked at me, pleased because we had found someone who never got flowers. We ran right over to the North Farm pasture and picked a bouquet of heather and brought it down to the barn. Oscar was pushing a wheelbarrow full of manure which he was going to throw on the compost heap behind the barn.

'Here are some flowers for you, Oscar,' we said and handed him the bouquet.

Oscar thought at first that we were having a joke with him, and wouldn't take the bouquet until we said he *had* to take it. A little while later Anna and I were hunting for a rabbit that had got out of its cage, and we walked by the compost heap. There lay Oscar's bouquet!

'I'm beginning to think Miss Johnson is wrong,' said Anna. So we decided to stop making people happy.

But a little later that afternoon Anna and I came into our kitchen and found a man sitting there. He was Mr Swenson from Stubby Point, and he looked very ill at ease. He had come to buy a pig from us, and my brothers had gone to get Father, who was ploughing the big field. Mr Swenson sat waiting in our kitchen.

Anna looked at him and then pulled me into a corner and whispered, 'Don't you think he looks bashful and uncomfortable? Why don't we try just once more. Let's speak kindly to him, the way Miss Johnson said.'

So that's what we decided to do. Usually Anna and I can talk nineteen to the dozen, but now, when we wanted to speak kindly to Mr Swenson to make him happy, we couldn't think of a thing to say – not a single word.

I thought and thought, and finally I said, 'It's a wonderful day, isn't it?'

Mr Swenson didn't answer, so I tried to talk to him once more.

'It's a beautiful day, isn't it?' I said.

'Uhuh,' said Mr Swenson.

Then I was silent. After a while I said, 'Yesterday was a beautiful day also.'

'Uhuh,' said Mr Swenson.

I looked at Anna because I thought she could help me a little.

Anna said, 'Tomorrow will probably be a beautiful day too.'

'Uhuh,' said Mr Swenson.

Just then Father came across the yard, and Mr Swenson got up to join him. But when he had just gone out of the door he poked his head back in, grinned, and said, 'And what was the weather like the day before yesterday?'

'Perhaps we made him a little bit happy, anyway,' said Anna later.

'Perhaps,' I said, 'but I've had enough. I'm not going to make any more people happy.'

But we did, all the same, because the next day Miss Johnson told us that Martha, a girl in our class, wasn't coming back to school for a long time. She was very, very ill and had to stay in bed several months. That night, before I went to sleep, I lay awake thinking about Martha, and then I decided to give her Bella, my most beautiful doll. This was because I knew that poor Martha hadn't got any toys at all.

In the morning when I told Anna that I was going to give Martha my doll, she went to get her nicest story book. And after school we went over to Martha's house. She was in bed

and looked very pale. Never have I see anyone as happy as Martha was when we put Bella and the story book beside her pillow and told her that she could keep them both. My goodness, how happy she was! She hugged Bella and the story book and laughed and laughed. Then she called her mother to come and see her presents.

When we were outside the door, I said to Anna, 'Isn't it funny, now we've made someone happy without even trying.'

Anna looked surprised and said, 'You're right! We have!'

And then she said, 'It was a lucky thing that we didn't start singing for Martha, because I think it makes people happier to get dolls and books.'

'Children, anyway,' I said.

If you have enjoyed this book and would like to know about others which we publish, why not join the Puffin Club? You will receive the club magazine, *Puffin Post*, four times a year and a smart badge and membership book. You will also be able to enter all competitions. For details send a stamped addressed envelope to:

The Puffin Club, Dept. A
Penguin Books Limited
Bath Road
Harmondsworth
Middlesex